BRIDGE
WITH

THE TIMES

BRIDGE
WITH

THE TIMES

Jeremy Flint

COUNTRY LIFE
BOOKS

To my wife, Honor,
without whose encouragement these articles would
never have been written and without whose industry this
book would never have appeared.

Published by Country life Books
an imprint of Newnes Books, a Division
of The Hamlyn Publishing Group Limited
84-88, The Centre, Feltham, Middlesex, England

ISBN 0 600 36894 7

Printed in Great Britain

Contents

Preface

There was no evidence of the dark clouds of economic uncertainty that surrounded the newspaper's future in September 1980 as I sat in the spacious offices of *The Times* in Printing House Square. I was there as one of many applicants to see John Higgins, then editor of the Saturday section, for the vacant post of bridge correspondent.

The interview had gone well, and I thought I detected a note of approval when Higgins asked how I would tackle the job. I replied: 'Combine reporting with occasional instruction, but place variety and entertainment above everything else.' Then came the thunderbolt.

'I play only the occasional game of bridge myself,' said John Higgins. 'How do you class yourself as a player?'

As I answered the question, I could not help feeling all was lost. Naturally, I had hoped that the emphasis would be on skill and renown as a player, rather than prowess with the pen. Rashly, I ventured: 'It must be a daunting task for you to make a selection in a field which is foreign to you.'

'We have our little ways', Higgins replied.

To my considerable surprise, I received the appointment. My father's pride would be exceeded only by my English master's astonishment, I thought to myself.

Some months later John Higgins, who has become a much respected friend, invited me to lunch at the Garrick Club. He reminded me of my quip about his 'daunting task'.

'It amused me', he said. 'It had the same impulsive foolhardiness as the charge of the Light Brigade.'

ONE

Round the World with 52 Cards

Bobby Fischer, the eccentric chess genius, made a considerable fortune from the brouhaha that surrounded his controversial match for the world championship against Boris Spassky in Reykjavik. It is also true, if less known, that the present world chess champion, Anatoly Karpov, is also a millionaire. With few exceptions, the leading bridge players have gained no great material rewards from their skill.

At least in my case a rich compensation has been the opportunity to travel the world playing my favourite game. In addition to almost every country in Europe, I have played in India, Japan, Hong Kong and Dubai. In 1966 I travelled 30,000 miles across the United States and Canada. My travels have also taken me to Rio de Janeiro, Buenos Aires, South Africa, and the Middle East.

Perhaps my most surprising experience occurred in India. As I gazed awestruck at the luminous perfection of the Taj Mahal, an Indian voice enquired: 'Excuse me, are you not Jeremy Flint the bridge player?' Flattering for me possibly, but a reminder of how difficult it must be for the genuinely famous to travel incognito!

I have included these articles in this book partly to underline that bridge is now a topic of world-wide attention.

A spine-chilling 'plot'

Competitive bridge has no official close season, but it is true that in the summer the game assumes a holiday atmosphere. July and August are the months to break unsuccessful partnerships and optimistically start again, with a new partner and fresh team-mates. The constancy of some established pairs makes a sharp contrast with the changeability of the more mercurial players who form a fresh liaison with the abandon of Hollywood's most fickle beauties.

In days gone by, a large contingent of British players used to go to all the major French congresses, Juan-les-Pins, Cannes and Deauville, where playing one leisurely session a day left time to enjoy the sun, the sea, and the excellent French food. Unhappily, the recession has forced many to substitute the jellied eels of Brighton for the *langoustines* of Deauville.

Although it was many years ago, I shall never forget my first experience of Juan-les-Pins. Tony Priday and I had decided to drive down. On the eve of the tournament Priday, by nature gastronomically un-adventurous, had ordered his very first artichoke. Despite my cries of horror he started to eat the spines. Priday was sceptical.

'You're pulling my leg', he said, as he carefully rejected the heart and continued to eat the spines with apparent relish. Predictably he suffered a very violent stomach-ache.

The conditions of the pairs provided that after three days of qualifying the field should be split into three separate competitions. Furthermore, all the competitors would carry forward a substantial percentage of their score.

For these first three days an ashen-faced Tony grasped his stomach in anguish, desperately seeking a remedy from the local chemists. Hardly surprisingly, we qualified third in the bottom section. Without being immodest, because of the carry-over we were now in the position of a classic winner receiving weight in an undistinguished maiden plate. With Tony restored to health, it was predictable that we should win this event against modest opposition by five clear tops. To make matters worse, we also won the open teams of four. The French, convinced that our performance was a dastardly plot, were not amused, and our appearance at the prize-giving was greeted with Gallic *froideur*.

Here is a hand that Priday played when the effects of the artichoke had worn off.

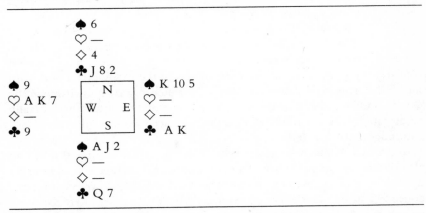

♠ 7 6
♡ 10
◇ A Q J 9 7 6 4
♣ J 8 2

♠ 9 8
♡ A K 7 6 5
◇ 10 8 5 2
♣ 9 4

N W E S

♠ K 10 5 4 3
♡ J 3 2
◇ Void
♣ A K 10 5 3

♠ A Q J 2
♡ Q 9 8 4
◇ K 3
♣ Q 7 6

	West	North	East	South
Pairs North-South game				*Priday*
Dealer South	—	—	—	1 NT
	NB	3 NT	NB	NB
	NB	—	—	—

Opening lead: ♡ 6

Priday won the first trick with the ♡Q. Aware that the French regard the weak no trump as a provocation to bid on any old tram tickets, he decided to play for the maximum by assuming that if West had ♡AK xxx together with the ♠K he would have ventured two hearts. He played the ◇K, overtaking with dummy's ◇A. (Notice that playing a small diamond to the Queen blocks the suit). The successful finesse of the ♠Q was followed by the marked finesse of the ◇9. Priday ran the diamonds to arrive at this five-card ending.

♠ 6
♡ —
◇ 4
♣ J 8 2

♠ 9
♡ A K 7
◇ —
♣ 9

N W E S

♠ K 10 5
♡ —
◇ —
♣ A K

♠ A J 2
♡ —
◇ —
♣ Q 7

On the last diamond, East was in trouble. In the vain hope that West had the ♣Q, he discarded the ♣K. Priday discarded the ♠2, finessed the ♠J and drove out the ♣A, making 12 tricks and scoring an outright top.

13

Doubled in Dubai

It was ten o'clock in the morning. I was sitting at a bridge table in a magnificent chandeliered ballroom. Facing me was a gentle looking man in crisp white Arab robes and head-dress.

'I am Sultan A. Haider' he said. 'May we play five card majors and a weak no trump?'

I pinched myself, but it was no dream. I was in Dubai, playing in the United Arab Emirates International Congress, and this was the first hand of the individual tournament.

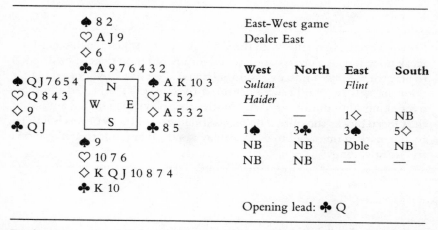

```
            ♠ 8 2
            ♡ A J 9
            ◇ 6
            ♣ A 9 7 6 4 3 2
♠ Q J 7 6 5 4                ♠ A K 10 3
♡ Q 8 4 3        N           ♡ K 5 2
◇ 9          W       E       ◇ A 5 3 2
♣ Q J            S           ♣ 8 5
            ♠ 9
            ♡ 10 7 6
            ◇ K Q J 10 8 7 4
            ♣ K 10
```

East-West game
Dealer East

West	North	East	South
Sultan		Flint	
Haider			
—	—	1◇	NB
1♠	3♣	3♠	5◇
NB	NB	Dble	NB
NB	NB	—	—

Opening lead: ♣ Q

Declarer won the club lead in hand and played the ◇K which I won with the ◇A. Drowsily I cashed the ♠K, on which my partner dropped the ♠7. Calculating that if declarer had only one club he would automatically be defeated, whereas if he had two the contract would be impregnable, I continued with the ♠A.

In practice it did not matter what I did *after* cashing the ♠K. I had already lost my opportunity. The only successful defence was to return a heart at trick two. Unable to re-enter his hand, declarer would be forced to concede a heart. The effect of cashing a spade was to resolve declarer's communication problems. As Shakespeare said in a different context: 'Weariness can snore upon the flint.' I like to delude myself that I might have found the defence a little later in the morning.

The tournament was generously sponsored by many local firms and in particular by Pakistan International Airlines and Hyatt Regency Hotels. Apart from a $10,000 first prize for both the teams and the pairs, an extensive list of prizes to a total value of $100,000 made this by far the most richly endowed bridge event of all time.

The bridge authorities of America and Great Britain have maintained an unswerving opposition to money prizes, arguing that to permit them would encourage chicanery and acrimony. It is especially pleasant to record that the appeals committe in Dubai was hardly needed and the referee did not even have to blow his whistle.

In the invitation team knockout, the organizers' sophisticated plans for Bridgerama went a little awry when Belladonna, Garozzo, Sheehan and I were narrowly defeated by Pakistan in the first round. This was the hand that was largely responsible for our downfall, with the bidding in our room.

♠ A K J 10 8 6		Love all
♡ A K 2		Dealer North
◇ Void		
♣ A Q J 4		

♠ 7 3		♠ 5 4 2	**West**	**North**	**East**	**South**
♡ Q J	N	♡ 7 5 3		*Sheehan*		*Flint*
◇ Q 9 8 6 2	W E	◇ K J 10 5 3	—	2♣	NB	2◇
♣ K 8 7 3	S	♣ 10 5	NB	2♠	NB	3♡
	♠ Q 9		NB	5◇[1]	NB	5♡
	♡ 10 9 8 6 4		NB	6♣	NB	6♡
	◇ A 7 4		NB	NB	NB	—
	♣ 9 6 2					

Opening lead: ♣ 3

1 Agreeing hearts and showing a diamond void – obviously discouraging news for South.

With an apparently inevitable heart loser I could not afford to reject the club finesse. When the ♡QJ dropped I made 13 tricks.

In the other room, Pakistan reached seven hearts. The declarer, Zia Mahmood, also received a club lead. Naturally he was appalled when he saw dummy. He took the first trick with dummy's ♣A, for in seven hearts the clubs are irrelevant. Painfully aware of the improbability of finding the ♡QJ alone, he conceived a plan which in practice might substantially increase his chances of success.

He returned to hand with a spade to lead the ♡8 intending, if West played low, to finesse. When Garozzo covered the ♡8 with the ♡J, Mahmood was forced to cash the ♡A, and pray.

'Imagine my thoughts when Garozzo covered', Zia said later. 'I thought he must be a mind reader. After all, how did he know that I did not have six hearts?'

But let Garozzo have the last word.

'With three hearts I would most certainly have covered the ♡8. Both from the bidding and Belladonna's play of the ♠2 on the first round I knew that South had only two spades. Provided I covered the ♡8 declarer would be unable to return to hand to repeat the heart finesse, as then he would have no entry to his spades.'

In pursuit of masterdom

The director pinned the results of the Master Pairs on the notice board. The young girl took one look and burst into tears. Noticing that a Mrs Bellamy had lost the title by a narrow margin, I tried to console her.

'That was very bad luck, Mrs Bellamy.' The girl looked at me blankly.

'My name's not Bellamy. That's me', she said, pointing to 17th place on the offending sheet. It was my turn to be bewildered.

'I only needed two master points to become a Life Master', she explained, 'and I missed it by a measly quarter of a point'. I partially consoled her with the thought that her enrolment would only be shortly deferred.

This remarkable incident in the spring of 1966 in Richmond, Virginia, gave me an insight into the passion with which American players pursue master points. The McKenney Trophy is awarded annually to the player who wins the most master points. In 1966 the winner was Peter Pender with a score of 1,282. In 1980, the winner, Ron Anderson, scored a staggering 2,725. Without wishing to detract from the winner's performance, it must be acknowledged that master points seem to have been caught up in the inflationary circle. Today, there are no fewer than 30,000 American Life Masters, nearly one in eight of all the registered members of the American Contract Bridge League. The trouble with that, as W.S. Gilbert put it is:

When everyone is somebodee
Then no–one's anybody.

We also have master points in Great Britain, where the number of points required to earn Life Master status is 300, as in America. There are only 370 British Life Masters, and 36 Grand Masters. The explanation for the wide difference lies in the 'rate of exchange' between American and British master points. The former are approximately four times easier to acquire. But even in England, the rank of Life Master may be a tribute to persistence and longevity, rather than a mark of excellence.

Although master points produce a handsome revenue for the ruling body, the short-comings of the system can be seen by comparison with the chess world. They too have their grades of ascending merit. But to reach the prestigious rank of Grand Master at chess there is an extra variable: the strength of the opposition. As bridge players cannot earn master points at European championships or invitation events, it follows that master points are no yardstick to measure players of championship class.

Unquestionably one of the most prolific master point winners of all time is Barry Crane. He has won the McKenney Trophy a record five times. When I played with Pender in 1966, the McKenney was our principal objective. I vividly remember the duels we fought with Barry Crane as we trekked through Wyoming and Colorado playing in towns whose names are more familiar to Western lovers than bridge players. On this hand, Crane proved too quick on the draw for us.

♠ K 10 8 4	Pairs	East-West game
♡ J 6 5 2	Dealer West	
◇ K 8 7		
♣ 5 4		

West	North	East	South
Pender		*Flint*	*Crane*
1♡	NB	2◇	NB
2♡	NB	NB	2♠[1]
Dble[2]	NB	NB	NB[3]

West hand: ♠ Q J 9 3 ♡ K Q 10 9 4 3 ◇ 2 ♣ K 3

East hand: ♠ 6 2 ♡ 8 7 ◇ A Q J 9 3 ♣ Q 10 8 2

South hand: ♠ A 7 5 ♡ A ◇ 10 6 5 4 ♣ A J 9 7 6

Opening lead: ♡Q

1 Crane played with a variety of partners. On this occasion he evidently felt that the advantage of playing the hand himself outweighed the greater flexibility of an informatory double.

2 This would be inexcusable at teams. Playing match point pairs, you cannot afford to let non-vulnerable opponents 'pick your pocket'.

3 At this point many players would seek refuge in three clubs. Crane's decision to stand his ground is instructive. Although West probably has four spades, it is almost equally certain that East has length in clubs. With his singleton heart, Crane hoped to be able to score two ruffs with his small spades.

Crane won the opening lead with his ♡A and immediately established a cross ruff position by playing the ♣A and the ♣7. Pender switched to his singleton diamond, which I won with the ◇J. In an attempt to cut down the ruffs, I returned the ♠2 on which Crane played the ♠5, Pender the ♠J and dummy won with the ♠K. Crane ruffed a heart in hand. He continued with a club on which Pender discarded a heart and dummy ruffed with the ♠8. When Crane ruffed a heart with his ♠A, we could not prevent Crane from scoring his seventh trick by ruffing another club in dummy.

Practically every other East-West pair had been allowed to play peacefully in two hearts, making at least 110. By defeating the contract by one trick, we salvaged some self-esteem, but no match points.

On this side of the Atlantic, Martin Hoffman is acknowledged to be an outstanding exponent of this method of scoring.

This hand, which Hoffman played in the Brussels heat of the Phillip Morris European Cup, deceived the majority of the declarers.

♠ K 10 8 7 6		Pairs	North-South game
♡ Void		Dealer East	
◇ 5 4 3 2			
♣ 10 9 6 5			

		West	**North** **East** **South**
			Schapiro *Hoffman*

West	North	East	South
		Schapiro	Hoffman
—	—	2♡¹	2♠
4♡	4♠	5♡	Dble
NB	5♠	NB	NB
Dble	NB	NB	NB

♠ Q 5 2   ♠ Void
♡ K 7 6 4   ♡ A J 9 8 5 3
◇ J 10 (W E)   ◇ Q 9 7 6
♣ A Q 4 3   ♣ 8 7 2

♠ A J 9 4 3
♡ Q 10 2
◇ A K 8
♣ K J

Opening lead: ◇ J

1 Weak two-bid.

Hoffman's choice of the simple overcall may seem conservative. But as he says it is often good tactics to introduce the long suit when there is the prospect of a competitive auction.

Hoffman won the ◇A, cashed the ♠A and finessed the ♠10. It appears natural to cash dummy's ♠K to extract the defence's last trump, but Hoffman foresaw the snag. When he plays on clubs, West wins the ♣Q and plays a heart, forcing dummy to ruff. Declarer continues with a second club to his King which *West ducks*. After that defence, declarer will be a trick short. Hoffman attacked the clubs before drawing the third round of trumps. With that vital extra entry in dummy, the defence could no longer prevent him from establishing the clubs.

Clash of the brightest stars in the East

The combined generosity of the Saturday Club in Calcutta and the Dunlop company was responsible for the lavish hospitality at the splendid tournament held under the aegis of the West Bengal Bridge Federation.

The principal event was a teams contest in which 13 leading Indian teams were joined by representatives from Bangladesh, Indonesia and Pakistan. The presence of Indonesia, winners of the Far Eastern Championships, and Pakistan, runners-up in the World Championships, ensured that the competition would be keen. The 16 teams played a complete round robin from which the leaders qualified for the semi-finals and a 64-board final. At every stage a large and appreciative audience watched the play on vu-graph, and the whole event received a gratifying response from the press.

This hand from the round robin featured a clash between some of the most colourful players in the competition:

```
            ♠ A K Q 5                 Game all
            ♡ A K Q 10 4              Dealer North
            ◇ 10
            ♣ Q 7 6
♠ J 6                 ♠ 10 3 2         West    North   East    South
♡ 8 5 3      N        ♡ 9 7 6 2        Mahmood Rubi Roy Masood  Gosh
◇ K 6 4 2  W   E      ◇ A 9 8 7 3       —      1♣      NB      2♣
♣ K 8 4 2    S        ♣ 9              NB      2♡      NB      2♠
            ♠ 9 8 7 4                  NB      3♠      NB      4♠
            ♡ J                        NB      4 NT    NB      5◇
            ◇ Q J 5                    NB      6♣      NB      NB
            ♣ A J 10 5 3              NB      —       —       —
```

Apart from the opening bid of one club, the rest of the sequence was natural. Zia Mahmood deduced that North-South were missing an Ace, very possibly the ◇A. He was just about to lead a small diamond when he remembered Garozzo's tip in the Bols Competition: 'Against slams you must *attack*'. Zia led the *King of Diamonds*.

The effect was devastating. Any lead but a diamond would have presented the contract immediately. The lead of a low diamond would have permitted declarer to establish a diamond for his twelfth trick. As it was, he could not escape from taking the losing club finesse.

Pakistan reached the final, where they met an Indian team captained by Anand Mekta. This hand had a critical effect on a close match.

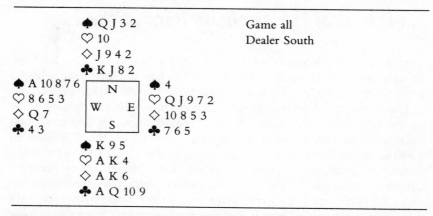

```
              ♠ Q J 3 2           Game all
              ♡ 10                Dealer South
              ◇ J 9 4 2
              ♣ K J 8 2
♠ A 10 8 7 6  ┌─────────┐  ♠ 4
♡ 8 6 5 3     │    N    │  ♡ Q J 9 7 2
◇ Q 7         │  W   E  │  ◇ 10 8 5 3
♣ 4 3         │    S    │  ♣ 7 6 5
              └─────────┘
              ♠ K 9 5
              ♡ A K 4
              ◇ A K 6
              ♣ A Q 10 9
```

When Pakistan sat North-South, they reached the inferior contract of six no trumps on a bidding sequence which has been lost or 'expurgated'. As the cards lie, the superior contract of six clubs would doubtless have been defeated by a spade ruff.

Masood (South) received the lead of the ♡3. Even if the spades were favourably distributed, Masood recognized that he would need some further assistance from the diamond suit in the shape of a singleton or doubleton ◇Q. If East has the doubleton Queen, there is no problem, as the suit will provide four tricks, so Masood correctly directed his play on the assumption that West had the Qx of diamonds. He played a spade to dummy's ♠Q, returned to his hand with the ♣Q and played the ♠9, covered by West's ♠10, and won by dummy's ♠J. When Masood cashed his clubs, West discarded a spade and the ♡5, while East parted with the ♡2 and the ♡Q. Before cashing the ◇AK, Masood cashed the ♡K. If Gokhale (East) had not been alert, Masood's play would have succeeded, because he would have subsequently put East on play to lead into dummy's diamond tenace. But on the ♡K East smoothly discarded the ♡9.

The Indian pair in the other room were content with the game, so they gained 12 IMPs, where but for accurate defence they might have lost 13 IMPs, a substantial part of the Indians' ultimate 30 IMP advantage.

20

Whimsy leads to victory

The jacaranda trees in full bloom provided the English tourists with a vivid reminder that they had exchanged English winter for South African spring. The team, consisting of Mr and Mrs G.C.H. Fox, I.N. Rose, R. Brock and my wife and myself, had travelled as the guests of the Friends of the Springbok Association to play a series of eight exhibition matches and some multiple teams events. A superficial assessment of the tourists' unbeaten record might suggest that South African bridge is a little below international standard. But that would be unfair. The main bridge centres are many miles apart and, unlike most other things in South Africa, air travel is expensive. The best players are distributed between Johannesburg, Pretoria, Cape Town and Durban, with the effect that we never met a team of representative calibre.

The itinerary started in Johannesburg with two exhibition matches and a Swiss Teams event. On this hand from the second match, you may think that we had the best of the luck when we gained a big swing from our whimsical bidding.

	♠ A 7 3			North-South game	
	♡ A K Q 2			Dealer West	
	♢ 10 9 4 3				
	♣ A K				

				West	**North**	**East**	**South**
♠ K 2		♠ Q 10 9 8 5 4		*Rose*	*Cope*	*Flint*	*Mervis*
♡ 10 9 8 7	N	♡ 6 5		NB	1♡	1 NT[1]	Dble
♢ 8 5	W E	♢ Q 7 6		NB	NB	2♣	Dble
♣ 10 9 7 6 3	S	♣ J 2		NB	NB	2♢	Dble
	♠ J 6			NB	NB	2♠	NB
	♡ J 4 3			3♠[2]	NB	NB	4♢
	♢ A K J 2			NB	4♠	NB	5♢
	♣ Q 8 5 4			NB	6♢	NB	NB
				NB	—	—	—

Opening lead: ♠ K

1 The comic no trump – either strong, or weak with a long suit.
2 A dual-purpose bid, to consume bidding space and perhaps persuade the opponents that they have a shortage in the suit.

Mervis won the first trick with dummy's ace. Loath to rely on the diamond finesse, he cashed the ♢AK and attempted to dispose of his losing spade on the hearts. Unhappily for him, I was able to trump the

21

third heart and cash the ♠Q.

The next hand, a good test of technique, is from the Swiss Teams, in which we hit the front only in the final round.

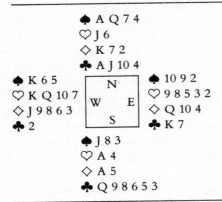

```
                ♠ A Q 7 4
                ♡ J 6
                ◇ K 7 2
                ♣ A J 10 4
  ♠ K 6 5          N        ♠ 10 9 2
  ♡ K Q 10 7   W     E      ♡ 9 8 5 3 2
  ◇ J 9 8 6 3      S        ◇ Q 10 4
  ♣ 2                       ♣ K 7
                ♠ J 8 3
                ♡ A 4
                ◇ A 5
                ♣ Q 9 8 6 5 3
```

South plays in five clubs on the lead of the ♡K. It may be tempting to take the club finesse, but there is a superior line. Win with the ♡A, and finesse the ♠Q. Then play three rounds of diamonds, ruffing the third in hand. Play the ♣Q to invite an unwary cover, win with dummy's ♣A and put West on play with the ♡Q.

After a match in Pretoria, the team travelled to Cape Town with a stop at Kimberley. It was here that Rose made one of his best decisions of the tour. While the rest of the team went to inspect the famous disused mine, Rose preferred to sun himself by the swimming pool. His lack of curiosity was singularly well-judged.

Riding on the crest of a Cape wave

Cape Town is as beautiful as people say; breathtaking scenery, a cool breeze to temper the sun, and well made wines at £1 a bottle. Unluckily, we arrived before the citrus fruit season, so the team settled on guava juice for its breakfast tipple. After some delightful days on the uncrowded beach, it was back to business with two exhibition matches against the Cape Town players.

In the first match, we met C. Bosenburg and Shirley Murray, a young and very promising pair. On this hand, Murray uncharacteristically missed a small but illuminating clue.

```
                ♠ J 7 6 4              North- South game
                ♡ 8 6 5               Dealer West
                ◇ A 7
                ♣ A J 8 4
    ♠ 8 2              ┌─────────┐    ♠ 10 9 3
    ♡ Q 2              │    N    │    ♡ K 10 9
    ◇ Q J 10 9 6 5 4   │ W     E │    ◇ K 8 3 2
    ♣ Q 2              │    S    │    ♣ K 9 3
                       └─────────┘
                ♠ A K Q 5
                ♡ A J 7 4 3
                ◇ Void
                ♣ 10 7 6 5
```

West	North	East	South
Flint	*Bosenb'g*	*Rose*	*Murray*
2♣[1]	NB	2◇	Dble
NB	3◇	4◇	4♡[2]
NB	NB	NB	—

Opening lead: ◇J

1 Either a strong hand or weak three diamond opening.
2 Pass would be more prudent, allowing North to introduce *his* four-card major.

Murray won my lead of the ◇J with dummy's ◇A. Rose played the ◇8 and she discarded the ♣5. After the finesse of the ♡J lost to my ♡Q, she ruffed my diamond continuation and cashed the ♡A. She then played four rounds of spades. Rose, who could not afford to ruff as he would be end-played, discarded a diamond. When Murray put him on play with the ♡K, Rose got out with his last diamond. She ruffed this and played a club to dummy's knave and Rose's King. Rose had no option but to return a club. Murray 'misguessed', contributing the ♣10, and lost the setting trick to Rose's ♣9.

The clue appeared on the first trick. If Rose had held the ♣KQx he would surely have played a discouraging diamond to invite me to find a club switch.

After two days in Port Elizabeth, we flew to Durban, our last port of call. The warmth of the Indian Ocean tempted even the more timid swimmers into the water. But any hungry shark would have had to swim in very shallow waters indeed to have caught them.

Petra Mansell, a member of the South African women's team which won the silver medal in the 1972 Olympiad, was commentating on our match against the Durban team. She was quick to spot a slight imperfection by Rose on this difficult hand.

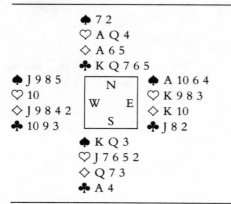

```
              ♠ 7 2
              ♡ A Q 4
              ◇ A 6 5
              ♣ K Q 7 6 5
♠ J 9 8 5        N        ♠ A 10 6 4
♡ 10       W         E    ♡ K 9 8 3
◇ J 9 8 4 2              ◇ K 10
♣ 10 9 3         S        ♣ J 8 2
              ♠ K Q 3
              ♡ J 7 6 5 2
              ◇ Q 7 3
              ♣ A 4
```

Playing in four hearts, Rose (South) received the lead of the ◇4 which East won with the ◇K. If East had cashed the ♠A there would have been no story, but he gave Rose a chance by returning the ♠4. Rose won and finessed the ♡Q, which spelt instant defeat.

On deep analysis, this was an error. If the hearts are 3-2 there is no problem, so declarer must address his mind to the 4-1 break. If Rose had won the ♡A and returned a heart towards his ♡J, East must duck, otherwise he loses a trump trick. Declarer can then turn to clubs, disposing of his two losing spades when that suit breaks 3-3. If West had the four hearts, the avoidance play would be to cash the ♡A, return to hand with the ♣A and play a heart towards the ♡Q.

Is there any reason to play East for the heart length rather than West? Yes. From the lead of the ◇4, and East's return of the ♠4, it appears that West has length in diamonds and four spades. The extra chance of the 3-3 club break would be a mirage if West also had the long hearts. So perhaps Rose might have found the winning line, but how many players would?

An American Who's Who

The McKenney Trophy is awarded annually to the player who wins the most master points in American competitions. It may be compared with the biggest winner on the American Golf circuit, with one small but significant difference. The golfer wins several hundred thousand dollars, the bridge player does not win a nickel.

If one studies the list of previous winners, it reads like a Who's Who of

American bridge. Charles Goren won the McKenney eight times, Oswald Jacoby four. In recent years the McKenney has become a specialist event because to hold any chance of success a player must devote an enormous amount of time, and, dare I say it, a considerable sum of money, in the ceaseless quest for master points.

Barry Crane won the McKenney for the first time in 1952. Ever since he has always been the man to beat, and on five occasions his skill and determination have proved too great for the remainder of the pack to catch him.

Henry Francis, in the Boston Herald American, described the 1981 fight for the trophy as 'one of the bitterest dogfights in the history of contract bridge'.

Crane, who is a well known television director, found that the strikes which disrupted the industry in the spring enabled him to devote his energies to bridge. But this was no one-horse race. Mel Skolnik, a successful businessman, but hitherto unknown in the bridge world, decided to make an all out attempt to win the 1981 McKenney Trophy. He employed former winners Soloway and Andersen to oversee the operation. The full list of Skolnik's 'army' was formidable indeed including world champions Meckstroth and Rodwell, and a host of other leading American players.

The bitterness between the two antagonists was forged in May. Rumour has it that Crane had originally offered to help Skolnik in his assault upon the McKenney, but had changed his mind. With seven months of competition still remaining, Crane and Skolnik were no longer on speaking terms. They were both so desperate for points that they would play in the early morning pairs, starting at 8.45 am, and the late night events ending at 3 am.

The Skolnik camp showed their expert planning by selecting the non-smoking division for their man, while injecting some professional pairs in the smoking division to make life more difficult for Crane.

The script for the final confrontation in Reno might have been written by Alfred Hitchcock.

Skolnik had a healthy, but not insuperable, lead of 137 points. In Reno, Crane won two big pairs events and was second in a third, to score 138 master points. But Skolnik, assisted by a powerful team, won the knock out teams, collecting 59 points. Crane's gallant attempt to cut back the deficit fell short by 58 points.

Skolnik rightly describes the McKenney as a bridge marathon compared with the normal sprint which a world championship entails. He obviously feels it is a prize well worth winning, for it is estimated that it cost him $250,000 to win.

This example of Crane's incisive defence justifies Skolnik's policy of employing his heavy artillery.

♠ 8 7 6 4	Pairs Game all
♡ 9 4 3 2	Dealer South
◇ Q 5	
♣ K J 4	

West	North	East	South
Crane			
—	—	—	1 NT[1]
2◇	2NT	NB	NB
NB	—	—	—

West: ♠ Q 9 2 ♡ J 5 ◇ A J 10 9 6 4 ♣ A 3

East: ♠ K 10 3 ♡ K 8 6 ◇ 8 7 ♣ 9 8 7 6 2

South: ♠ A J 5 ♡ A Q 10 7 ◇ K 3 2 ♣ Q 10 5

Opening lead: ◇J

1 15-17 points.

The raise to two no trumps in this sequence should be construed as strictly competitive, carrying no invitation to proceed. Crane led the ◇J which declarer covered with dummy's ◇Q. East signalled with the ◇8 to show that he had at most a doubleton. Declarer played a low heart to his ♡10 losing to Crane's ♡J. The pedestrian defence of establishing the diamond would suffice to beat the contract by one trick, but that is not the way to win a pairs event.

Crane correctly deduced that declarer's play of the ♡10 marked him with the ♡AQ. If he had the ♣Q, together with the ◇K which he was known to hold, he could not hold both the Ace and King of spades because that would make 18 points, too strong for an opening of one no trump by his methods.

Accordingly Crane switched to a spade, but unlike his less gifted counterparts, not a small spade but the ♠Q. If declarer had won with the ♠A, Crane would have taken the first round of clubs and put his partner in with the ♠K to obtain a diamond return for a three-trick penalty. Declarer wisely ducked the ♠Q, and Crane returned to the establishment of his diamonds to earn a fine score of + 200.

TWO

Polyglot or 'Polyrot'

Artificial systems and conventions are an endless source of controversy. The system lovers, I believe, would be quite happy to dispense with the play of the cards as a needless interruption to their beautifully contrived manoeuvres. But there is a world of difference between artificial systems and a sensible interpretation of natural bidding. The one depends on codes, the other on logic.

There was a time when I was a devoted system bug. But my attempts to attract a wider audience to play and watch bridge have persuaded me that complicated systems do deter people from watching the game. It is too late, even if it were desirable, to eliminate the artificialities from international bridge. That would stifle 'progress'. But it is not too late to organise more tournaments where the competitors play only simple conventions and do not need a bridge lexicon.

All systems go

Like stiletto heels and baggy trousers, bridge systems enjoy a vogue. The intense rivalry that once enlivened British bridge certainly stemmed from the loyal and vehement claims of the exponents of the different methods. When Vanderbilt introduced contract bridge, most of the players played the Vanderbilt club. Before the war, nearly everybody played one of the popular one-club systems. But in the immediate postwar period the Acol team, by their writing and sparkling example, converted the majority of British players to two-club systems. I vividly remember how scornful Harrison-Gray was about the Italian systems, the Neapolitan and the Roman Club.

Despite the Blue team's success in the late 1950s, British prejudice against the Italian one-club systems was so entrenched that for several years their use in domestic competitions was forbidden. Eventually, in the mid-1970s, their opponents could no longer pretend that the only merit of the Italian systems was their very unfamiliarity.

Now I sense that the pendulum may swing back once more. In a recent conversation, Garozzo confided: 'Playing one-club systems when your side is vulnerable and the opponents are not is a waste of breath. Nowadays everyone comes into the bidding on rubbish, obstructing the beautiful scientific sequences that I have taken years to devise. It is very sad,' he concluded mournfully, as if he were a classical guitarist watching a pop group.

The Italian influence was also responsible for another lasting change. The success of their featherweight overcalls has persuaded practically all the leading players to imitate this aggressive style of intervention.

All overcalls, however weak, should have a considered objective. Sometimes the simple one-level overcall may be a constructive attempt to buy the contract at either part score or game level. Again with more distributional hands, it may be good tactics to suggest a sacrifice with a low-level intervention. But obstructive overcalls are made for an entirely different reason. To overcall one club with a bid of one diamond does not deprive the opposition of any bidding space. On the other hand, a butt in of one spade can disturb the opponents constructive bidding.

It was the inconvenience of this one spade overcall which inspired the American expert Alvin Roth to invent the Sputnik or negative double, in an attempt to minimize the effect of this disruption.

Finally, there are lead directing or strategic overcalls, which if employed with discretion can either make the defence easier or pose problems for the opposition in the bidding.

My first hand illustrates the dangers of the pointless overcall.

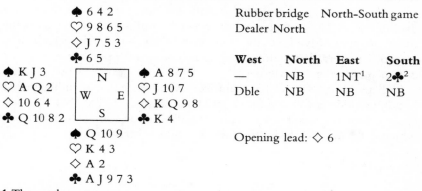

	♠ 6 4 2		
	♡ 9 8 6 5		
	♢ J 7 5 3		
	♣ 6 5		

Rubber bridge   North-South game
Dealer North

West	North	East	South
—	NB	1NT[1]	2♣[2]
Dble	NB	NB	NB

Opening lead: ♢ 6

1 The weak no trump.
2 'I had fourteen points, partner – surely I am entitled to say something?'

It was a massacre. The defence took three heart tricks, three spade tricks, a diamond and three trump tricks, to inflict a 1,400 penalty. In my opinion, South got what he thoroughly deserved. The overcall had no lead directing value. After his partner had passed, there was no possible prospect of North-South bidding a game. If he were lucky, South might make a part score, but the obvious risk of entering the bidding with a broken suit made the bid totally unsound.

To overcall on the next hand would not occur to many players, but East had an excellent motive for his unorthodox bid.

	♠ A K Q		
	♡ 8 5 2		
	♢ J 8 4		
	♣ A Q 9 8		

Pairs   Love all
Dealer West

West	North	East	South
NB	1♣	1♢	1♡
NB	1♠	NB	3♣
NB	3♡	NB	4♡
NB	NB	NB	—

East took his three diamond tricks, and later scored a trump trick to defeat the contract. A plus score was sufficient to give East-West a complete top on the board, as every other North–South pair made at least 10 tricks in no trumps.

East's primary purpose for his unorthodox intervention was to secure a diamond lead. The advantage of the possible confusion it might cause for the opposition outweights the slight risk of this one-level overcall. It is rare for an overcall at the one level to be doubled for penalties unless the opponents have good trumps.

Perhaps North should have bid 3◇ over 3♣, but it is unlikely that South would have felt that his ◇9 5 2 were adequate to bid 3NT. It is fair to give East the credit for creating the illusion of a long diamond suit which deflected North–South from the right contract.

Beware boomerangs

'Don't pre-empt with a weak partner' is a sound rubber bridge maxim. Obviously, any penalty you concede will be in a poor cause. But a greater deterrent is that pre-emptive bids, designed to disrupt the opposition, all too frequently boomerang.

To select the best response to a pre-emptive bid requires judgement, vision, and a sound knowledge of the language of bidding. Imagine that your partner, at love all, has opened three hearts. What action would you recommend with these three hands?

A	B	C
♠ K Q 4	♠ A K 6 3	♠ J 4 2
♡ 8 7 2	♡ 8	♡ A Q 7
◇ Q J 6 3	◇ A Q 5 2	◇ A K 4 3 2
♣ K Q 2	♣ A K 7 3	♣ A K

A. The worst bid is three no trumps. Of course, with a helpful lead and a benign distribution, you will sometimes succeed, but too infrequently. Four hearts is also over-optimistic. The only sensible call is no bid. It is a simple matter of valuation.

B. It's amazing how many bridge players who have played the game all their lives still bid three no trumps. Any sensible reconstruction of partner's hand will demonstrate that four hearts will be a good contract. Three no trumps will vary from poor to putrid.

C. This is more difficult. If your partner has the right cards, there might well be a slam. Normally a pre-emptive bid should not contain an outside Ace, so Blackwood will be singularly unrevealing. The correct technique is to cue bid your lowest control, four clubs. Your partner should appreciate that you are interested in a slam but have no spade control. If he has a spade control, it is up to him to take the initiative.

To underline the points I have made, here is a typical hand on which your partner might have opened three hearts.

♠ 5
♡ K J 10 9 6 5 4
♢ 9 8
♣ J 10 5

The competitive bidding which follows a pre-emptive bid often requires delicate judgement.

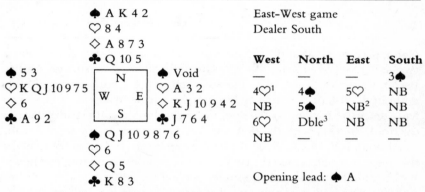

	♠ A K 4 2			East-West game			
	♡ 8 4			Dealer South			
	♢ A 8 7 3						
	♣ Q 10 5			**West**	**North**	**East**	**South**
♠ 5 3		♠ Void		—	—	—	3♠
♡ K Q J 10 9 7 5		♡ A 3 2		4♡[1]	4♠	5♡	NB
♢ 6		♢ K J 10 9 4 2		NB	5♠	NB[2]	NB
♣ A 9 2		♣ J 7 6 4		6♡	Dble[3]	NB	NB
	♠ Q J 10 9 8 7 6			NB	—	—	—
	♡ 6						
	♢ Q 5						
	♣ K 8 3			Opening lead: ♠ A			

1 Despite the vulnerability, the quality of the hearts fully justifies the intervention.
2 Relying on his partner to choose between doubling and bidding six hearts.
3 Unwise. Without the ♣Q, indefensible. Six spades must be a cheap insurance.

North followed a poor decision in the bidding with a lamentable display in the defence. Declarer ruffed the spade in dummy and returned to his hand with a trump. When he continued with a diamond, North panicked, taking the trick with the ♢A. Hoping that South had two hearts, he forced the dummy with the ♠K. Declarer was able to cash the Ace of trumps and dispose of his losing clubs on the ♢K and the ♢J.

North should have had no difficulty in forming a picture of West's hand. Surely the only hope of defeating the contract must lie in the club suit. If North ducks the ♢A, declarer loses no diamond but cannot avoid the loss of two club tricks.

On the next hand, the protagonists were all players of world championship class. It was France v USA — the final of the 1980 World Olympiad.

31

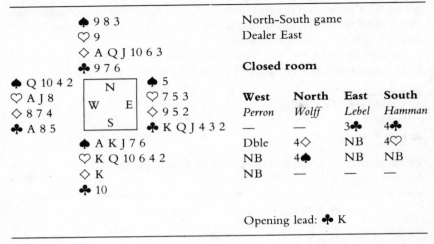

♠ 9 8 3
♡ 9
◇ A Q J 10 6 3
♣ 9 7 6

♠ Q 10 4 2   ♠ 5
♡ A J 8   N   ♡ 7 5 3
◇ 8 7 4 W   E   ◇ 9 5 2
♣ A 8 5   S   ♣ K Q J 4 3 2

♠ A K J 7 6
♡ K Q 10 6 4 2
◇ K
♣ 10

North-South game
Dealer East

Closed room

West	North	East	South
Perron	*Wolff*	*Lebel*	*Hamman*
—	—	3♣	4♣
Dble	4◇	NB	4♡
NB	4♠	NB	NB
NB	—	—	—

Opening lead: ♣ K

Good players invariably use the cue bid of four clubs to describe a two-suiter. This explains North's amendment to four spades. Notice Perron's double of four clubs. He was subtly suggesting a penalty double without the risk of doubling and finding his partner trickless. If Lebel had had a defensive trick he would doubtless have doubled four spades. Perron overtook the ♣K with the ♣A and forced dummy with a second club.

Although Wolff suspected the bad trump break, he had to try to make the contract, so he cashed the two top trumps, confirming the bad news. Wolff could have gone one down by playing the ♡K; instead he tried to take heart discards on dummy's diamonds. Perron was able to ruff the fourth diamond, cash the ♠Q and wait for two heart tricks. Two down. 200 to France.

Open room

West	North	East	South
Soloway	*Mari*	*Rubin*	*Chemla*
—	—	3♣	4♣
5♣	Double	NB	NB
NB	—	—	—

Opening lead: ♠A

The bidding started in the same way, but Soloway's attempt to maintain the barrage misfired badly. Possibly five clubs is not a bid of which he is particularly proud. On the contrary, North's double showed excellent judgement. No doubt Mari reasoned that as South's bid was based on a major two-suiter, his diamonds would be more valuable in defence than attack. Chemla had no difficulty in finding the diamond switch, so the French extracted a 500 penalty to add to the 200 they had earned in the closed room.

A swing of 12 IMPs to France.

Pope was not a bridge player, but how aptly he wrote:

Tis with our judgements as our watches, none
Go just alike, yet each believes his own.

When average meets expert

If two average players cut together against two of the club's experts, what are the odds against the weaker pair winning the rubber? Certainly not more than 11–8, and provided that the experts are not a practised partnership, 5–4 would probably be a more accurate estimate. A practised partnership is a different proposition. It is irrelevant that the experts would not be permitted to play their pet system; their greater understanding of many bidding and defensive situations, unrelated to systems, would give them a considerable advantage.

The hand below demonstrates the fallibility of two internationals playing in an unaccustomed partnership.

		♠ Void		Rubber bridge	Love all	
		♡ 7 2		Dealer South		
		◇ A K Q 9 8 7 6				
		♣ J 5 4 3				
♠ Q J 10 8			♠ A 9 7 4 3	**West**	**North**	**East**	**South**
♡ A 9 4 3	N		♡ K J 6 5	—	—	—	NB
◇ 10 5 3	W E		◇ Void	NB	1◇	Dble	1NT
♣ K 7	S		♣ A Q 10 8	Dble	NB	NB	NB
		♠ K 6 5 2				
		♡ Q 10 8		Opening lead: ♠ Q		
		◇ J 4 2				
		♣ 9 6 2				

The experts were sitting East–West. Before describing their follies, one must admire North's courageous pass of one no trump doubled. West led the ♠Q. East, immediately recognizing the futility of allowing declarer to obtain the lead, took the ♠A and correctly switched to a club. Unhappily, he selected the ♣Q. Now the defence could only make six tricks.

In the post-mortem it was West who took the initiative, politely drawing East's attention to the fatuity of playing the ♣Q and continuing with the gentle suggestion that his pass of one no trump doubled was equally uninspired. East, after pleading guilty to the defensive error, mounted a strong counter attack on the question of the bidding. He claimed that his pass of one no trump doubled was eminently correct. To justify his double, West's hand should have contained some values in diamonds which would be useless in attack but invaluable in defence.

East's most forceful observations were reserved for West's double, which he colourfully described as the 'pursuit of fairy gold at the cost of an honest income'.

Whoever was the more to blame, this cameo explains why I would prefer to take the odds rather than lay them.

I have noticed that doubles of 1 NT are a source of constant confusion. It might be helpful to suggest some general guidelines.

The double of an opening no trump is a penalty double. I have always believed in keeping these doubles up to strength, that is to say 17 points, or 16 with a good lead. It is a popular fallacy to suppose that you need less strength to double 1 NT in the protective position, because then you do not have the advantage of the opening lead.

The next hand illustrates a common misunderstanding.

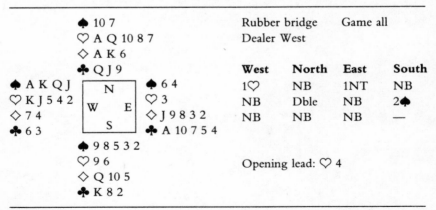

	♠ 10 7				Rubber bridge	Game all	
	♡ A Q 10 8 7				Dealer West		
	◇ A K 6						
	♣ Q J 9						

West	North	East	South
1♡	NB	1NT	NB
NB	Dble	NB	2♣
NB	NB	NB	—

West hand: ♠ A K Q J ♡ K J 5 4 2 ◇ 7 4 ♣ 6 3

East hand: ♠ 6 4 ♡ 3 ◇ J 9 8 3 2 ♣ A 10 7 5 4

South hand: ♠ 9 8 5 3 2 ♡ 9 6 ◇ Q 10 5 ♣ K 8 2

Opening lead: ♡ 4

Declarer finessed the ♡Q and played the ♠10. West had noticed his partner's revealing ♡3 on the first trick, so after winning the ♠10 with the ♠J he continued with the ♡K, which was covered by North and trumped by East. Nothing could prevent the defence from making the ♣A and three more trump tricks. North was not pleased. He claimed that his delayed double of 1 NT was a penalty double, which South had no justification to remove.

This is correct. If a player passes a suit bid on his right and subsequently doubles a bid of one no trump by either opponent, the double should be treated as a penalty double, coupled with the request to lead the suit bid on his right.

'By taking out my double into your moth-eaten spade suit, you turned a profit of five hundred into a loss of a hundred', North concluded.

'Two hundred', interjected West mildly. 'I had a hundred honours.'

Aging acolytes

The Acol system was 'born' more than 40 years ago in an obscure club in Acol Road, Hampstead. The club has vanished, but the brain child of the unlikely combination of the academic Marx and the bohemian Simon still retains its immense popularity.

In 1937, the original Acol team of Harrison-Gray, Macleod, Marx and Simon carried all before them, showing no respect for the accepted authorities of the day. Not surprisingly, this uninterrupted series of victories antagonized their rivals. Kenneth Konstam disdainfully described Gray's goal of 'Par bridge' as dull and uncreative. The Acolytes had the last word. Macleod replied with a clerihew neatly lampooning the folly of constantly trying to be brilliant.

Acol was rightly described as more a state of mind than a system. The system, such as it was, revolved round a weak non-vulnerable no-trump and a well-defined intermediate two bid. But it was the easy-going philosphy of 'bid what you think you can make, and pass when you like' that distinguished the Acol team from the practitioners of more hide-bound methods.

To what extent has Acol changed over the years? Almost beyond recognition. You might as well compare the liberalism of Gladstone with the current policies of the Liberal Party. Consider this example of an early Acol triumph:

West	East	Bidding	West	East
♠ K J 4	♠ A 10 9 8		1 ♡	2 ♣
♡ A J 9 8 6	♡ 2		2 ◇	2 ♠
◇ A 10 7 4	◇ 5 3		NB!	
♣ 2	♣ A 10 9 6 4 3			

Nothing could stop East from making eight tricks on cross-ruff lines. Oh for the uninhibited joys of youth! No Acol player would pass two spades today. 'Park where you like' is now controlled by traffic wardens and police. The absence of rules has been sensibly modified to recognize that some sequences must be forcing without placing the players in a doctrinal strait-jacket.

Part of the credit for the reshaping of the system must be given to the Sharples brothers. After incessant research and numerous adaptations, they conclusively demonstrated that their supercharged version of Acol was an accurate bidding weapon indeed.

Two elements of Acol have stood the test of time, the weak no trump and limit bids. Even the Americans, once wedded to forcing jump raises, have adopted limit raises in a major. Many systems use the weak no trump, notably the Precision Club. But the Acol two bid, originally regarded as the flagship of the system, no longer enjoys the same esteem.

There are, I believe, several good reasons for this. Before I discuss the objections, here is an example which shows the advantages of the Acol two bid:

West	East	*Bidding*	West	East
♠ A K Q J 10 8	♠ 9 3		2 ♠	2 NT
♡ A J 10 7	♡ K 6 5		3 ♡	4 ♠
◇ A 2	◇ Q 7 6 4			
♣ 6	♣ J 8 7 2			

East, because of West's rebid of three hearts, can appreciate the value of the King of hearts. Coupled with the assurance that West has promised eight playing tricks, East makes the imaginative but correct bid of four spades. Of course, if East bids only three spades, West should pass. Very neat, but I regret somewhat infrequent, and that is my first objection.

To use three valuable bids, two spades, two hearts, and two diamonds, to introduce comparatively rare hands is theoretically unsound. In the early days many players mistakenly thought that any hand with eight playing tricks qualified as an Acol two bid. But to open two diamonds with this hand is purposeless and misleading:

♠ A 7 2
♡ 4 2
◇ A K Q 7 6 5 4
♣ 3

Reese tried to correct that fallacy by defining the Acol two bid as a hand of 'power and quality'.

In *The Acol system of Contract Bridge* he gave this example:

♠ A J 7 6 5 3
♡ 4
♢ A K 2
♣ A K 5

Now I totally agree that if you open one spade and everyone passes, you will have an anxious moment waiting to see if you have missed game. Reese's claim that a two level response would embarrass the one spade opener is no longer valid, because most good players play the rebid of three spades after a two level response as forcing. The main objection to opening two spades is the danger of finishing in the wrong strain.

Let us suppose that your partner has one of these two hands:

A   **B**
♠ 8   ♠ 8
♡ A 7 3   ♡ 7 6 3
♢ 10 9 6 5 4 3   ♢ Q J 6
♣ Q 7 3   ♣ Q J 10 9 8 6

I suspect that the Acol sequence would be identical with both hands:

2 ♠   2 NT
3 ♠   NB

A miserable substitute for six diamonds on (A) or six clubs on (B).

It is my profound belief that it is nearly always wrong to open an Acol two bid with a hand that is *playable in three suits*. If one accepts the unorthodox proposition that a two club bid is only forcing to three of a major, then *two clubs* would be my choice of opening bid.

Notice that this would take the bidding no higher opposite a weak hand, but would lead to a game or slam when partner has a fair hand with strength in the minors.

My final objection to the Acol two bid is based on the belief that there are better uses for the bid. Many players have already adopted the multi-coloured two diamonds, and a few use both two hearts and two spades as multi-purpose bids. I remember Harrison-Gray's look of outrage when I suggested that we should play the Roman two diamonds to introduce powerful three-suiters. I wonder what he would make of these new-fangled toys.

To bid or not to bid, that is the question

Much has been written about *playing* with the odds, little about *bidding* with the odds. Some bridge writers tend to suggest that there is always a right or a wrong bid. In real life, it is not so simple. I am going to describe three hands, all of which were held by Britain's leading international players. Before I tell you what they bid and how they fared, perhaps you would like to consider what you would have done, bearing in mind that you are playing with an expert partner. You are South in each case.

	N	
W		E
	S	

♠ A
♡ Q 9 7 6
◇ 8 6 5
♣ A K Q 9 7

I. Multiple teams   Love all
Dealer North

West	North	East	South
—	NB	4◇	?

	N	
W		E
	S	

♠ K 7
♡ K 10 8 6 5
◇ Q J
♣ J 8 4 3

II. Rubber bridge   Love all
Dealer South

West	North	East	South
—	—	—	NB
NB	1NT[1]	2♠	3♡
3♣	NB	NB	?

1 12-14 points.

	N	
W		E
	S	

♠ Void
♡ 5
◇ Q 9 8 7 5 4
♣ Q J 8 6 5 4

III. Teams of four   East-West game
Dealer North

West	North	East	South
—	1♠	NB	?

I. There are several possible calls. No bid, double, five clubs, and four hearts. At the table, South bid a confident four hearts. This was the case that he made for this apparently daring bid: 'To pass would be supine; a double would be ill-judged, as it would undoubtedly produce four spades. This leaves four hearts and five clubs. As East has opened four diamonds and I hold three, North may well be short in diamonds, which in turn increases the chances that he will have four hearts. If the wind blows in the shape of a sharp double from West, I can still retire to five clubs.'

You may consider that it was a lucky choice, but it worked well in practice when North produced:

♠ K 10 8 4 3 2
♡ A J 8 4
♢ 10
♣ J 5

II. South doubled, arguing that North would appreciate that his double was co-operative and remove it if appropriate. There are several flaws in this argument. Three hearts was a doubtful bid in the first place, and this motley collection does not justify any further enterprise opposite a typical weak no trump. Co-operative or not, a penalty double with only two trumps is unsound. Not surprisingly, three spades doubled was made with an overtrick. A retreat to four hearts by North would have cost 300.
III. There are three possible bids: one no trump, pass, and two diamonds. Two diamonds could succeed, but is much more likely to carry the boat over the rapids. One no trump may seem a distortion, and there is much to recommend a pass. But the main virtue of a pass, which is that the opponents will re-open and allow you to express your hand with an unusual no-trump bid, disappears if you think too long before making your decision. In the second round of the British Bridge League Trials, South after some reflection passed, only to find that five diamonds was unbeatable and one spade unmakeable.

Taking out an option

Fashions change in the defence to pre-emptive three bids. Twenty years ago, most rubber bridge players used three no trumps as a request for partner to bid, retaining the double in its punitive sense. British duplicate players generally used the 'lower minor'. Here three diamonds over three clubs and four clubs over any other three bid requests partner to bid; a double is for penalties, and three no trumps is natural.

The Americans, who have remained faithful to the optional double, considered three no trumps as cumbersome and the lower minor as over-contrived. Other methods have had their passing vogue from time to time.

Today, the majority of the experts on both sides of the Atlantic rely on the optional double. In truth, the word 'optional' is misleading, because the double is unequivocally intended as a 'take-out double'. Obviously, the doubler's partner may convert the bid into a penalty double if he has a powerful trump holding, or if he believes that the danger of bidding outweighs the risk of doubling the opponents into game.

The undeniable advantage of using a double for take-out is that it permits the bidding to subside at the three level. Playing duplicate pairs, it is fatal to allow your opponents to make a part score of three diamonds when your side can make nine tricks in either major. I suspect that this consideration partly explains why the Americans, who have always played more duplicate pairs than rubber bridge, found any method which forced the bidding to the four level unappealing.

But for the players with poor judgement, the double for take-out is as suitable a toy as a flick-knife for a child.

```
                  ♠ A Q 5 3           Rubber bridge    Game all
                  ♡ K Q 5             Dealer West
                  ◇ K 6 3
                  ♣ Q 6 2
    ♠ 2                      ♠ K J 10 4   West    North    East    South
    ♡ A J 10 9 8 6 4   N     ♡ 2          3♡      Dble     NB      3♠
    ◇ Q 4           W   E    ◇ A J 10 7 5  NB      4♣!      Dble    NB
    ♣ J 10 9           S     ♣ A 5 4      NB      NB       —       —
                  ♠ 9 8 7 6
                  ♡ 7 3                   Opening lead: ♣ J
                  ◇ 9 8 2
                  ♣ K 8 7 3
```

Declarer thanked his partner gruffly as he inspected dummy with ill-concealed distaste. He won the first trick with the ♣K, and played the ♠9, permitting East to win with the ♠10. East switched to his singleton heart, which West won with the ♡A. Recognising that a heart ruff would be unlikely to assist the defence, West shrewdly continued with the ♣10, which held the trick.

West made another good play when he switched to the ◇Q. Declarer covered with dummy's ◇K, losing to East's ◇A. East cashed the ♣A and two more diamond winners, before exiting with the fourth round of diamonds. Nothing could prevent East from taking two more trump tricks. Six down, 1,700 to East-West.

'I had sixteen points', said North apologetically, correctly sensing his partner's displeasure.

'Quite so', said South. 'In not redoubling, you showed admirable restraint.

This disaster contains a number of lessons in bidding after a pre-empt by the opposition. First, it is considerably more dangerous to enter the bidding when one opponent is unlimited. Secondly, an essential criterion for a take-out double is suitable distribution, which should include a shortage in the opponent's suit. Any defect in distribution must be compensated by greater strength in high cards. Thirdly, nothing could be more puerile than totting up the number of points regardless of their location. And finally, if North's double was bad, his bid of four spades was grotesque. A partner who makes a minimum response to a take-out double may reasonably be assumed to have six or seven points. But North, with five of his wretched 16 points in the opponent's suit, needs considerably more than seven points opposite his shapeless pudding to justify a further bid.

Pre-emptive bids create a minefield of uncertainty for both sides. Only one thing is sure. This particular North will make the same mistake again, but to make up for it, he will always inform you proudly of the number of points he had.

Artificially yours

Bridge books usually give a full account of opening bids, responses, and rebids. After the opener's rebid, the student is told, responder will usually be in a position to set the final contract. Quite true as far as it goes, but when responder is not in that happy position, some authors become remarkably coy.

I understand their dilemma. The innumerable sequences that can flow from responder's non-terminal second bid would require a disproportionate amount of space to cover them all.

Duplicate players have generally accepted the concept that the fourth suit is forcing and often artificial. But even experienced players are unsure of the forcing quality of some of the bids that follow.

West	East	Bidding	West	East
♠ A K J 5 3	♠ Q 10		1 ♠	2 ♣
♡ J 4 2	♡ 10 3		2 ◇	2 ♡
◇ A J 4 2	◇ K Q 10 3		2 ♠	?
♣ 5	♣ K Q J 9 2			

Most modern pairs would start like that, but what should East bid now? The answer is 3◇, which is forcing. Why? Because if East wished to make an invitational raise to 3◇, he would have done so directly without the interposition of the fourth suit. This should be the full sequence:

West	East
1 ♠	2 ♣
2 ◇	2 ♡
2 ♠	3 ◇
3 ♡¹	3 ♠²
4 ♠	NB

1 Having denied a full stopper by rebidding two spades, West can safely show his half stopper.
2 Similarly, East's holding of Q 10 is ample to justify his delayed support.

A simple enough hand, yet many pairs would languish in an impossible 3NT or in 5◇ with three top losers.
    This hand should present few problems:

West	East	Bidding	West	East
♠ J 10	♠ A Q 8 7 6 4		1 ♡	1 ♠
♡ A J 9 6 5 4	♡ K		2 ♣	2 ◇
◇ 2	♡ K 6 5 4		2 ♡	3 ♠
♣ A Q 7 4	♣ K 3		4 ♠	NB

Notice that 3♠ is forcing because East could have bid a non-forcing 3♠ available over 2♣, had he wished. But change the West hand to:

West	East
♠ J	♠ A Q 8 7 6 4
♡ A Q 10 9 6 5	♡ K
◇ 10 2	◇ K 6 5 4
♣ A J 10 9	♣ K 3

Now West has an opportunity to make an exceptionally subtle bid; over three spades, he bids 4◇, inviting East to choose the final contract. There can be no ambiguity, because West has followed a strictly limited sequence. East should appreciate that his ♡K has now assumed an extra significance and select the superior contract of 4♡.
    Sometimes there is no bid which accurately describes the strength and shape. This is a hand that the pundits avoid discussing:

West	East	Bidding	West	East
♠ A K 10 7 4	♠ 6 3		1 ♠	2 ♣
♡ 5 2	♡ Q 4 3		2 ◇	2 ♡
◇ A K Q 3	◇ J 10		?	
♣ 4 2	♣ A K Q J 7 6			

The bidding started easily but what should poor West bid now? No trumps without a stopper in hearts is taboo, a repetition of the spades at the two level too feeble, a jump to 3♠ an overstatement, and a 'preference' to 3♣ a distortion. That leaves 3◇, which at least possesses the merit of being forcing, and keeping the pot on the boil, even if partner supposes that it shows a five-card suit. The bidding will then proceed to the best contract in this way:

West	East
1 ♠	2 ♣
2 ◇	2 ♡
3 ◇	4 ♣
5 ♣	NB

West need not feel that his clubs are inadequate, especially as East has shown a good hand with no interest in either of West's suits.

Admittedly these fourth suit sequences are difficult, but here are two general rules to guide you through the maze.

● The fourth suit bidder promises a further bid except when the opener continues with 2NT.

● A raise after the fourth suit is forcing when responder could have made an invitational raise.

Blackwoodsmen

Easley Blackwood has written a number of books about bridge, but it is undoubtedly his eponymous convention which has earned him world-wide recognition. Surprisingly, the bridge world's original reaction was a mixture of scorn and disinterest. The editor of the magazine to whom he submitted his manuscript returned it with a curt rejection slip, and the leading experts of the day dismissed it as a childish prop for novices. My predecessor, Edward Mayer, who disliked all conventions, invited the Portland Club to agree that the convention violated rule 23, which provides a harsh penalty for an honour card 'exposed during the auction'.

No doubt Mayer's submission was prompted by his mordant sense of humour. It is just as well that it was overruled, for otherwise thousands of bridge players would have been deprived of their favourite toy.

For many years, the experts obstinately refused to recognize the worth of the convention. Even the Acol team, dedicated apostles of direct bidding insisted on the retention of the Culbertson four-five no trump convention. Today that convention is used as frequently as wooden-shafted golf clubs.

In the modern game, over 90 per cent of all bridge players use Blackwood and over 80 per cent misapply it. The principal objection to the convention was that the Blackwood bidder became an automatic interrogator, asking questions but revealing nothing. It was a superficial objection, as we shall see.

The average player mistakenly assumes that Blackwood should be the automatic prelude to any slam. The expert will only use the convention on roughly one slam hand in three.

Never forget that Blackwood is only a good convention when harnessed to intelligent cue-bidding. Until a partnership has established that it possesses first or second round control in every suit, it is a bad mistake to introduce Blackwood. It follows that when a good player bids a conventional four no trumps, he shows that the partnership controls every suit.

Common sense reveals two other occasions where the four no trump bidder shows as well as asks. If the agreed trump suit is clubs, it is obviously unsound to use Blackwood with fewer than two aces, as a five diamond response would take the partnership too high. Similarly, if diamonds are the agreed trump suit, the four no trump bidder promises at least one ace.

It would be absurd to search for a grand slam missing an ace. So if the four no trump bidder follows with a bid of five no trumps, he promises that the partnership holds all the aces. Sometimes this knowledge will permit the responder to bid the grand slam in preference to giving his conventional response. Although most players retain five no trumps to ask for kings, there is considerable merit in the modern practice of using five no trumps as a trump enquiry.

This hand is a good test of bidding.

Rubber Bridge
Game all   Dealer West

West	East	Bidding	West	East
♠ A Q 7 4	♠ K J 2		2 NT	3 ♡[1]
♡ Q 10 3	♠ 9 8 7 6 5 4		3 ♠[2]	5 ♡[3]
◇ A K J 4	◇ Void		NB[4]	
♣ K Q	♣ A J 9 7			

1 Stronger than four hearts and leaving space to exchange information about controls.

2 A cue bid. West correctly chooses to show the control which conserves the maximum bidding space. The cue bid is doubtful because for all his 21 points, West's hand is badly put together.

3 A precipitate request to bid six hearts if West's trumps are good enough. I always recommend discounting knaves in the valuation of a hand for slam purposes. East can convey the same message with greater circumspection. If he bids four clubs and West continues with four diamonds, East can follow with four hearts, still leaving West in no doubt that East is concerned about the quality of the trump suit itself.

4 West understood the five heart bid, but as North held ♡KJ2 unhappily they were already one trick too high.

Notice that Blackwood would be a useless and cumbersome bludgeon on this delicate hand.

To show the other side of the coin, here is another hand from Rubber Bridge.

Rubber Bridge
Game all   Dealer West

West	East	Bidding	West	East
♠ Q 5 4	♠ K 8 3		1 ◇	1 ♡
♡ K	♡ A 8 7		2 ♣	4 ◇
◇ K 8 5 2	◇ A Q J 10 6 4		4 ♡	4 ♠
♣ K Q 9 7 6	♣ 10		4 NT	5 ♣
			5 ◇	6 ◇

East-West were playing Canapé, that is to say the second suit bid is presumed to be longer than the first. After four diamonds, four hearts, four spades, and five clubs were all cue bids. Four no trumps was not Blackwood but a general slam try, which certainly appears to be an overstatement of West's strength. It is easy to see that Blackwood would have saved the partnership from the indignity of bidding a slam missing two Aces.

I am delighted to say that North-South had no difficulty in defeating the slam. This may appear uncharitable, but the hand has a history. It was 1970; East-West were none other than Belladonna and Garozzo, Cansino and I were North-South, and we were playing a challenge match for £100 a hundred.

Learning to sign off correctly

Most people would agree that it is rude to finish a telephone conversation without saying goodbye. Yet many bidding exchanges end equally summarily with one partner vainly crying 'hello, hello, hello'! The rebuff is not calculated. It arises from an ignorance, or at least a difference in interpretation, of the language of bidding.

All bridge bids may be classified into three types; sign off, invitational and forcing. It may help to consider them as carrying the same messages as a set of traffic lights. The sign off is red — you must stop. Invitational or limit bids — you may proceed with caution. Forcing bids are green — you must go on.

A member of my club, using his favourite catch phrase, assures me that 'at the vicarage' there is no such thing as a sign off. I know what he means. Here are two examples of sequences where West is required to pass.

(1) West	East		(2) West	East
1NT	2 ♡		1 ♣	1 ♠
			2 NT	3 ♣

There is a similarity. In each case West has made a limit bid (1NT and 2NT). Despite the precise information at his disposal, East has decided to subside in a part score. His decision should be respected.

Limit bids should convey a picture of the assets of the hand within a defined range. All no trump opening bids and raises to 2NT fall into this category and so do jump raises in a major or a minor.

(1) West	East	(2) West	East
1 ♠	3 ♠	1 ♣	2 NT

West is invited to continue if he has any extra values.

In standard bidding systems any opening bid of one of a suit is invitational, which partner with a very weak hand may pass. All pre-emptive bids carry the same message; my strength is mainly distributional, concentrated in the suit that I have bid. Do not expect any outside high cards, especially aces. Many players have adopted the so called gambling 3 No Trumps opening, which promises a solid seven-card minor with no outside king or ace. It is less generally understood that the onus for placing the contract rests on the 3 No Trumps bidder's partner. Here are two hands which underline the point. On each, East has opened 3 No Trumps, and you have to respond as West.

(1)	♠ A K 3 2	(2)	♠ A K Q J 4
	♡ 10 4 3 2		♡ K 5
	♢ Q 4 3 2		♢ A J 8 7 2
	♣ 6		♣ 5

(1) It may be tempting to pass, gambling that the defence will find the wrong lead. That would be unsound. The correct reply is 4 Clubs, which conclusively places the final contract.

(2) Obviously, this hand is strong enough for a slam. To protect the ♡K from attack, the right bid is 6 Clubs.

Forcing bids provoke the most controversy and misunderstanding. Immediately after the war, the Acol team introduced their free and easy methods with spectacular success.

'Bid what you think you can make, pass if you feel like it', was their battle cry. The trend in recent years has been to treat more and more sequences as forcing.

For the benefit of 'the vicarage', all two bids are forcing, as are any responses in a new suit (except by a passed hand). All reverses should be treated as forcing, except after a 1NT response. Today, nearly everyone will treat all the following sequences as forcing, although some diehards may have their reservations about (B).

A		B		C		D	
West	East	West	East	West	East	West	East
1 ♠	2 ♣	1 ♣	1 ♠	1 ♣	1 ♠	1 ♠	2 ♣
2 NT	3 ♠	2 ♢	3 ♣	2 NT	3 ♣	3 ♣	3 ♠

The complications and forcing quality which follow the introduction of the artificial fourth suit are limitless. But I suggest one simple rule. The fourth suit bidder should promise one more bid, except where the opener rebids 2NT, as in this example. West's 2NT guarantees a guard in diamonds, but only a minimum opening bid.

West	East
1 ♡	1 ♠
2 ♣	2 ♢
2 NT	—

If I have seemed to pontificate, the absurd bidding misunderstanding that follows may restore the balance. It occurred in the European Championships, Athens 1971 – Great Britain v Iceland.

Love all   Dealer East

	North		West	East
♠ 10 9 5		♠ A K 2	*Flint*	*Cansino*
♡ Void	N	♡ A K J 10	—	1 ♣[1]
♢ A K Q 10 7 6 4	W E	♢ 2	3 NT[2]	4 ♣[3]
♣ K 4 3	S	♣ Q 10 7 6 2	4 ♢[4]	4 ♡[5]
			NB[6]	—[7]

1 Precision Club, at least 16 points, any distribution.
2 Promises a solid suit with precisely one outside control (an ace or a king).
3 Asks for the outside control: 4 Diamonds would ask for the suit.
4 *Peccavi.*
5 To this day, I do not know why Cansino did not bid 6 Diamonds over 3 No Trumps. From his hand he could judge that my outside control must be in Clubs.
6 Perhaps stupidly, I formed this picture of Cansino's hand:

♠ K Q J
♡ A K Q J 10 8 7
♢ Void
♣ Q 7 6

7 'Hello, Hello, Hello'!

Iceland bid the hand to 6 No Trumps, only to find the diamonds divided 4-1. This excellent contract was defeated by three tricks. As Cansino made eight tricks in our ridiculous contract, we gained two IMPs on the board. Bridge can be a cruel game.

How a no-trumper can lead
with his chin

The weak no-trump has provoked many heated debates over the years. Experts of the old school point derisively at the large penalties that the bid sometimes incurs.

'If you stick your chin out by shouting that you have a weak balanced hand,' they argue, 'you deserve the crisp uppercut that you often get.'

But that is only one side of a possibly counterfeit coin. As Muhammad Ali demonstrated so ably, provided that you are quick on your feet, and able to duck and weave, you can sometimes afford to relax your guard.

Here is a typical scenario where the weak no trumper seems to be in trouble.

```
♠ A 2            N              Game all
♡ A Q 5      W       E         Dealer South
♢ A J 9          S
♣ K Q 10 8 5
              ♠ 10 9 6 3
              ♡ K 4 3
              ♢ K Q 2
              ♣ A J 9
```

South opens the bidding with a weak no trump, and West doubles. Here are four possible hands that North could hold.

A	B	C	D
♠ Q J 8 5	♠ K Q 8 7 2	♠ Q J 8 7	♠ K Q J
♡ J 10 9 8 6 2	♡ J 10 9	♡ J 10 9 8	♡ J 10 9
♢ 10 3	♢ 10 5 3	♢ 10 8 7 6	♢ 10 8 7 6
♣ 6	♣ 7 2	♣ 2	♣ 7 6 4

On (A) North retreats to two hearts. If West elects to double, a footsure defence can inflict a flesh wound by taking six tricks.

On (B), North escapes to two spades. If West doubles, he could rue the day. After the lead of the ♣K, the only continuation which does not present the contract at once is the Ace and another spade. Declarer plays hearts and even if West plays correctly by getting off play with a heart, he will still be in trouble in the end game.

On (C), if North were not vulnerable he might try the old gambit of responding two clubs! When this is doubled, he redoubles, and again

North-South find safe harbour in two spades. Vulnerable, two diamonds would be more prudent.

Finally on (D), West would do well to defeat the contract and the most probable result would be a plus score to North-South, either from one no trump doubled and made, or should East mistakenly remove the double, from an ungainly East-West part score.

It comes to this. Even when North-South are heavily outgunned, a retreat to a five-card suit may escape punishment or be unpunishable. Furthermore, there are several other shapes (e.g., 4-4-4-1) which allow the deft wrigglers to escape. It is only when North has a weak *balanced* hand that South is in trouble, and even then the adverse strength must be so distributed that one defender would double and his partner would pass.

Now for the other side of the picture. It is self-evident that one no trump has a greater pre-emptive value than any other opening bid. It puts a boot firmly into the enemy camp, frequently causing obstruction and sometimes inflicting casualties.

Maintaining the same South hand, study the problems that confront West when he has no clear-cut bid.

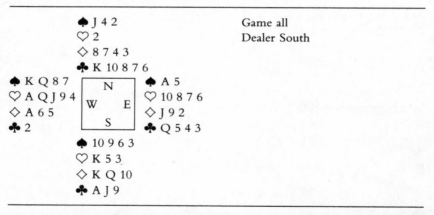

```
              ♠ J 4 2              Game all
              ♡ 2                  Dealer South
              ◇ 8 7 4 3
              ♣ K 10 8 7 6
 ♠ K Q 8 7   ┌──────┐   ♠ A 5
 ♡ A Q J 9 4 │  N   │   ♡ 10 8 7 6
 ◇ A 6 5     │ W  E │   ◇ J 9 2
 ♣ 2         │  S   │   ♣ Q 5 4 3
              └──────┘
              ♠ 10 9 6 3
              ♡ K 5 3
              ◇ K Q 10
              ♣ A J 9
```

Most Wests would double South's 1NT. It is true that East-West should reach four hearts without difficulty, but should East prefer the substance to the shadow by doubling North's retreat to two clubs, he would find the result unsatisfying.

The advocates of the strong no trump remind me of people who are afraid of flying. They forget that statistics conclusively prove that they are far more likely to be run over by a bus.

Two-suiters for all occasions

Powerful two-suiters are like a sharp knife. Handled with care, they can be invaluable, but a moment's clumsiness can spell self-destruction.

The first question the holder of a two-suiter should ask himself is: 'Am I going to try to judge the final contract myself, or shall I force my partner to make the final decision?' Here is a cautionary example of the latter technique:

	♠ 8 3			Rubber bridge	North-South game
	♡ K 2			Dealer East	
	◇ J 9 8 7				
	♣ 10 9 6 4 2				

				West	North	East	South
♠ 7 4 2	N	♠ 5					*Leslie*
♡ 5 4	W E	♡ 9 8 3					*Dodds*
◇ Q 5 3 2	S	◇ A K 10 6 4		—	—	1◇	2◇
♣ K J 7 5		♣ A Q 8 3		3◇	NB	3NT	4◇

		West	North	East	South
	♠ A K Q J 10 9 6	Dble	NB	NB	Redble
	♡ A Q J 10 7 6	NB	NB	NB	—
	◇ Void				
	♣ Void				

The late Leslie Dodds, an automatic choice for any British team in the 1950s, planned to correct his partner's anticipated club response with further diamond cue bids up to the six level. His desperate attempt to encourage her to place the correct value on her King of hearts if she happened to hold it, turned sour. The hand should have provided the *locus classicus* for a treatment suggested some years before by S J Simon.

Unhappily North developed the idea that South was trying to expose East's psychic bid. The concession of an enormous penalty was a poor exchange for the impregnable grand slam. Dodds took the reverse in good part, blaming himself for overestimating his partner's ability.

Suppose South had been the dealer. What is the best way for him to describe this wonderful major two-suiter?

The correct sequence would be:

North	South
—	2 ♠
2 NT	6 ♡

North is invited to bid to bid the grand slam if he has a high honour in either major suit. Before using the sequence, it is as well to make sure that your partner does not feel at liberty to pass an opening two bid if he has a yarborough.

Two-suiters can sometimes lead to wounding penalties when there is a misfit. This hand caused a spirited debate at the rubber bridge table.

```
                  ♠ Q
                  ♡ Q
                  ◇ K Q J 10 6 4
                  ♣ K 6 5 4 3
   ♠ K 9 7 5 2   ┌─────────┐   ♠ 10
   ♡ 10 9 8 3    │    N    │   ♡ K 2
   ◇ A 5         │ W     E │   ◇ 9 8 7 2
   ♣ Q 10        │    S    │   ♣ A J 9 8 7 2
                 └─────────┘
                  ♠ A J 8 6 4 3
                  ♡ A J 7 6 5 4
                  ◇ 3
                  ♣ Void
```

Rubber bridge   Game all
Dealer South

West	North	East	South
—	—	—	1♠
NB	2◇	NB	2♡
NB	3♣[1]	NB	3♡
NB	3NT[2]	NB	4♡
Dble	NB	NB	NB

Opening lead: ♡ 3

1 Asking for trouble. The danger of the misfit is already apparent. The sensible bid is three diamonds, with pass a plausible alternative.
2 Suicidal.

Note West's choice of the ♡3 as an opening lead, preserving the sequence intact. Unless East has an honour, the ♡10 will be irrelevant. East covered the ♡Q with the ♡K and declarer won with the ♡A. If at this point declarer had played a low spade, he would have saved a trick from the wreckage. As it was, he lost two hearts, four spades, and a diamond, to concede an unnecessary 1,100 penalty. Incredibly, it was North who took the offensive in the post mortem.

Often the onus of selecting the right contract will fall on the weak hand.

```
                  ♠ Q J 10
                  ♡ 8 7 6 5
                  ◇ J 8 4 3
                  ♣ J 2
   ♠ 6 5 4      ┌─────────┐   ♠ 3 2
   ♡ Q J 2      │    N    │   ♡ A K 9 4 3
   ◇ A 9 6 5    │ W     E │   ◇ K Q 10 7
   ♣ 8 7 3      │    S    │   ♣ A 4
                └─────────┘
                  ♠ A K 9 8 7
                  ♡ 10
                  ◇ 2
                  ♣ K Q 10 9 6 5
```

Teams   North–South game
Dealer East

Closed room

West	North	East	South
—	—	1♡	2♣
2♡	NB	3◇	3♠
4◇	4♠	Dble	NB
NB	NB	—	—

East's bid of three diamonds was a game try showing extra values. North reasoned that South must hold 11 black cards to justify his aggressive bidding at unfavourable vulnerability. To visualize that his subsidiary values in the black suits would be sufficient for game is the hallmark of a good player. There were no problems in the play. 790 to North-South.

In the open room, the bidding took the same course up to and including North's bid of four spades. But then East showed better judgement by bidding five diamonds. South led the ♠K, on which North contributed the ♠Q. South continued with two more rounds of spades, forcing East to ruff with the ♢7. East cashed the ♢K and paused to recapitulate the bidding.

To justify his bidding South must have 11 black cards, but was there any clue to indicate whether his shape was 5-1-1-6 or 5-0-2-6? Yes. If South had had a void heart, he would have underled his ♠A to obtain a heart ruff.

East crossed to dummy with the ♡J. He then confidently finessed the ♢10, and cashed the ♢Q. Dummy's ♡Q provided an entry to draw North's last trump. If South had switched to the ♣K or the ♡10 at trick two, the contract would have been unmakeable, but that does not detract from East's good judgement and fine play, which earned a swing of 14 IMPs.

Worth the sacrifice

At duplicate bridge it is simple to assess whether a sacrifice is a good proposition. If the penalty you suffer is less than the score your opponents would have made, the sacrifice is a demonstrable success, provided of course that the opponents would have made their contract.

Sacrifice bidding at rubber bridge introduces some additional considerations. This may explain why one expert at my club addresses a polite homily to all his partners outlining the follies of sacrificing, particularly with him.

If the opponents are vulnerable, and you are not, how many points can your side profitably concede in order to save the rubber? Duplicate players who are unaccustomed to playing rubber bridge are especially prone to arithmetical miscalculation. At duplicate, to lose five hundred to save the game at this vulnerability would be a success. At rubber bridge it is a downright failure. The odds remain 3-1 against you winning the rubber. There is a further less obvious disadvantage; if your opponents bid and make a slam, they will get a bonus of 750 points, whereas you will only get 500.

The existence of a part score should exert a powerful influence on your decision to sacrifice. With neither side vulnerable, it is good tactics to save the game if you have a part score and very unwise if the position is reversed. Sacrificing when the opponents are vulnerable and also have a part score is the privilege of the rich.

So far, we have assumed that the players are of equal ability. But let us suppose that you have cut the 'pond idiot' against two fair players. Do you really wish to prolong the struggle? It is amusing to watch players who should know better, putting up a spirited defence of their bed of nails, perhaps because they allow their conceit to get the better of their commonsense.

Making the decision to sacrifice at Duplicate is a good test of a players judgement.

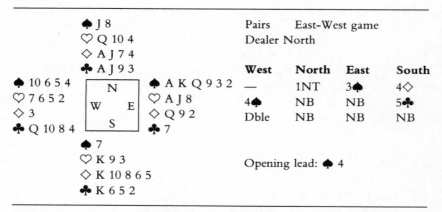

	♠ J 8		Pairs	East-West game		
	♡ Q 10 4		Dealer North			
	◇ A J 7 4					
	♣ A J 9 3					
			West	**North**	**East**	**South**
♠ 10 6 5 4	N	♠ A K Q 9 3 2	—	1NT	3♠	4◇
♡ 7 6 5 2	W E	♡ A J 8	4♠	NB	NB	5♣
◇ 3	S	◇ Q 9 2	Dble	NB	NB	NB
♣ Q 10 8 4		♣ 7				
	♠ 7					
	♡ K 9 3		Opening lead: ♠ 4			
	◇ K 10 8 6 5					
	♣ K 6 5 2					

The bidding is typical of the pairs game, with both sides contributing some aggressive bids. Possibly West hoped that the vulnerability would induce North-South to sacrifice. South's bid of five clubs can charitably be described as dubious.

East won the opening lead with the ♠Q, and continued with the ♠K, which South ruffed with the ♣2. Before playing to the third trick South tried to reconcile the aggressive bidding of his vulnerable opponents with the small number of high cards they possessed. He decided correctly that they must be relying on distribution. Accordingly, he cashed the ♣K and successfully finessed dummy ♣9! Now he played the ♡4, which East ducked, permitting South to win the ♡K. He finessed the ♣J and drew the last trump, discarding the ♡3 from his hand. Deducing that West must have a singleton to justify his four spade bid, South played a diamond to dummy's ◇A and bravely finessed the ◇10 to bring home a lucky, but skilfully played, contract.

54

The bidding on the next hand, from Rubber Bridge, reminds me of the senseless courage of the Kamikaze pilots.

	♠ A 10 7	Rubber bridge	East–West game
	♡ A K 9 8		and 60
	◇ J 7 3	Dealer West	
	♣ 10 8 2		

♠ J 4		♠ K 6 5 3 2
♡ Q J 10	N	♡ 7 4 2
◇ Q 9 6 4	W E	◇ A 10 8
♣ A K J 7	S	♣ Q 4

West	North	East	South
1NT	Dble[1]	Redble[2]	2♣[3]
Dble	NB	NB	NB

	♠ Q 9 8
	♡ 6 5 3
	◇ K 5 2	Opening lead: ♡ Q
	♣ 9 6 5 3

1 I have already described the imprudence of 'flag flying' at this score. The double of a weak no trump on inadequate values is an especially unsound gambit.
2 Without the part score the redouble would be unsound, as it would show at least 11 points. Here it is permissible because it creates a useful forcing situation, allowing either partner who has a good holding in trumps to double for penalties.
3 Technically inexcusable, but South knew his partner.

South won the lead with dummy's ♡K and continued with the ♡A and the ♡9. West won with the ♡J and switched to the ♠J. East took his ♠K and returned the ♠2. South could only hope that the defence would lose its way. He won the spade in dummy with the ♠10, and played the ♣2 which ran round to West's ♣7. West switched to the ◇4 which East won with the ◇A. Unwisely, East persevered with spades, playing the ♠3. West thought for some time before finding the correct defence. He ruffed with the ♣K and returned the ♣J, neatly avoiding the end-play. 'Why did you return the ♠2 instead of the ♠3?' West enquired, 'I nearly made a mistake'.

'Don't be so fussy,' East retorted, 'I played it the next time.'

Going on the transfer list

Every year, to the horror of the purists, the dictionaries recognize the existence of some new words, and it is only a matter of time before they attain widespread acceptability. Even Fowler's most ardent disciple would probable concede that no single word could evoke the instant horror of 'blitz-krieg,' and only those who detest all gallicisms would pretend that fashionable or smart captures the full sense of 'chic'.

Bidding is no dead language, either. The rules and ethics committee of the English Bridge Union spends untold hours limiting the endless proliferation of new systems and conventions. Many years ago, S.J. Simon suggested the proper test to judge a new convention: does it deprive you of a useful natural bid, and does it work?

Undeniably *transfer bids* fulfil both these qualifications. The whole range of responses to INT is considerably enriched at the negligible cost of dispensing with 2◇ as a weak take-out.

Let me start with an example which demonstrates how transfer bids can solve an everyday problem. East-West are using a weak no trump. West opens INT and this is East's hand:

♠ Q 4
♡ A J 7 6 4
◇ K Q 9
♣ 8 7 4

Whether this hand will produce a game opposite a weak no trump must obviously depend on how well the hands fit. Many players would respond 3♡ hoping for the best. Here are three hands which West could hold to justify his opening bid of one no trump:

A	B	C
♠ 10 8 3	♠ J 2	♠ A J 9
♡ K Q	♡ Q 5 3	♡ 8 5
◇ A J 10 8 4	◇ J 10 8 4 2	◇ A J 8 4
♣ K 5 3	♣ A K Q	♣ Q 6 5 3

On A, using standard methods, the bidding would be brief but ineffective.

West	East
1 NT	3 ♡
3 NT	NB

Unless the opponents were kind enough to lead a red suit, 3NT would fail by anything from one to five tricks.

This would be the sequence using transfer bids:

West	East
1 NT	2 ◇[1]
2 ♡ [2]	2 NT[3]
3 ◇[4]	4 ♡[5]
NB	—

1 Compelling West to rebid 2 ♡.
2 West may exceptionally rebid 3 ♡ with four hearts and a maximum no trump.
3 Notice the extra flexibility. East can paint an accurate picture of his hand, a balanced 11 or 12 points containing a five-card heart suit.
4 West appreciates the strength of his doubleton ♡ K Q and invites East to set the final contract. Of course it would be purposeless to show the diamonds unless West wanted his partner to make the final decision. His bid promises precisely two good hearts.
5 East draws the correct inferences. If his hearts had been weaker he would have settled for 3 NT.

Four hearts is an excellent contract which at worst depends on the position of the ♣A.

On B, standard methods would also prove inadequate.
The sequence would be:

West	East
1 NT	3 ♡
4 ♡	NB

One too high.

This would be the transfer sequence:

West	East
1 NT	2 ◇
2 ♡	2 NT
3 ♡[1]	NB

1 West recognizes that his weakness in spades together with his three-card support for hearts will make the heart part score a safer contract.

On C, standard methods will produce an absurdly over-optimistic contract.

West	East
1 NT	3 ♡
3 NT	NB

The transfer sequence is:

West	East
1 NT	2 ◇
2 ♡	2 NT
NB	—

Even 2NT may be one too many.

Here is the full schedule of responses to 1NT using transfer bids.

2♣ – Stayman.

2◇ – transfer to 2♡.

2♡ – transfer to 2♠.

2♠ – transfer to 2NT.

2NT – transfer to 3♣.

Bids at the three level are natural and invitational, but not forcing. For those who like the simple life 2 ♠ can be used as a straightforward transfer to 2NT. For the sophisticated player the response of 2♠ is used to initiate a Baron sequence. The purpose of the 2NT response is two-fold. The simple and most frequent use is to allow the partnership to rest in 3♣ or 3◇. If after

West	East
1 NT	2 NT
3 ♣	

East bids 3◇, that bid is terminal, signifying a weak hand with at least six diamonds. More ambitious players may use the 2NT response to resolve a recurrent dilemma. Suppose you hold:

♠ A 7 4
♡ 3
◇ A Q 10 7 6 4
♣ K 5 3

Your partner opens 1NT to which you respond 3◇; unhelpfully, he rebids 3NT. What do you do now? If you pass he might well hold:

♠ K Q 3
♡ J 7 4
◇ K 2
♣ A 9 8 7 2

so you go down in 3NT where 5◇ would present no problem. If you decide to press on to 5◇ you may find to your annoyance that his hand is

♠ J 10 9
♡ K Q 10
♢ K J 9
♣ Q J 10 4

5♢ stands virtually no chance, whereas 3NT is iron-clad. The 2NT transfer machinery allows you to judge instead of guessing. The sequence would start:

West	East
1 NT	2 NT
3 ♣	3 ♡

The bid of a major at the three level after this begining says, 'I have a singleton in the suit, but I have values for game, including a good six-card minor.' It becomes the opener's responsibility to select the contract.

Iain Macleod once wrote 'Bridge is an easy game'. Surely all these complications are inconsistent with that assessment? But the *tools* are all important. No doubt Nicklaus and Watson would have played golf well with wooden shafted baffies and cleeks but, I venture to suggest, not quite so well.

Bidding that amateurs find forbidding

'You're no better than a drug pedlar who gets up on a soap box to denounce the evils of narcotics.'

'What do you mean?' I enquired, somewhat abashed.

'You admit that you collaborated in the invention of the Little Major, the Multi-coloured two diamonds, competitive doubles and God knows how many other artificial devices.'

'Yes.'

'Now you trot round the country and defend the 'Sobranie Challenge' policy of forbidding one club systems and limiting all conventional gadgets. I put it to you', said my interrogator in a tone worthy of Marshall Hall at his most menacing, 'that it is dificult to imagine anything more hypocritical'.

I remain unrepentant. Here is the explanation for my apparent ambivalence. In the late 1950s and early 1960s, when the Italian blue team, using their artificial club systems, were virtually invincible, the English Bridge Union steadfastly refused to allow English players to use these methods. This was an obviously preposterous decision, effectively saddling British international teams with a self-imposed handicap.

Whether such systems convey an advantage in terms of accuracy remains debatable. But beyond question they are a deadly weapon against opponents unfamiliar with them.

Eventually wiser counsels prevailed, and British teams were allowed to play artificial systems. The trouble was, and is, that to be effective the international players must have frequent opportunities to practise. This means that the ordinary player will sometimes be confronted with bidding that he does not understand at all.

Rubber bridge players and many duplicate players have no patience with these complex codes. They argue that artificial systems are a dangerous distortion of an excellent game. And, to be fair, the increasing complexity of the bidding is certainly one of the reasons why live bridge enjoys such a relatively small following.

The solution as I see it lies in a deliberate division of bridge. Let the 'professionals' have their tournaments, and their international championships, where any intelligible system is permitted. But for the rest provide some tournaments where the bidding is limited to the absolute minimum of conventions.

This hand from a recent tournament would undoubtedly receive different treatment from rubber bridge players.

```
              ♠ Q 4
              ♡ Q 10 3                    Game all
              ◇ A Q 8 7                    Dealer South
              ♣ J 8 4 3
♠ J 10 9 8         N         ♠ 6 5 3
♡ 7 6 5 4                    ♡ K 8 2
◇ J 6 5 3     W       E      ◇ 10 9 2
♣ K               S         ♣ 10 9 6 5
              ♠ A K 7 2
              ♡ A J 9
              ◇ K 4
              ♣ A Q 7 2
```

West	North	East	South
—	—	—	1♣[1]
NB	1◇[2]	NB	1NT[3]
NB	2♠[4]	NB	2NT[5]
NB	3♡[6]	NB	4♣[7]
NB	4◇[8]	NB	4♡[9]
NB	4♠[10]	NB	6NT[11]
NB	NB	NB	—

Opening lead: ♠ J

Here is the explanation of an especially artificial variation of Precision.

1 Strong artificial.

2 8-15 balanced.

3 Interrogative.

4 8-11 points – no four-card major.

60

5 Interrogative.

6 2-3-4-4, shape precisely.

7 Beta control asking.

8 0-2 controls (an ace = 2, a king = 1).

9 Trump asking in clubs.

10 No top honour.

11 Wisely preferring no trumps because of the known frailty of the club suit.

On the lead of the ♠J the hand should present no problems to a good player. First finesse the heart, to judge whether to play the club suit for three tricks or four. When the heart finesse succeeds, declarer should play the ♣A because he can afford to lose one trick in the suit, but not two. Declarer's play did not match the precision of his bidding. He finessed the club and subsequently played for the wrong squeeze.

At rubber bridge I imagine the auction would be brief, simple and effective:

South	North
2 NT	6 NT

THREE

Dogberry and the Pests at the club

The faces and accents may differ between London and New York, but you will find the same generic types at every bridge club. The overbidders, the timid, the querulous, the gloaters and the moaning losers. And then there are the bores who insist on telling you about their triumphs, and worse still, their hard luck stories.

Rubber bridge is an essential part of the rich patchwork of the game. Technical skill alone will not guarantee success unless it is accompanied by psychology and considerable patience.

If there is a moral in these pieces, it is this: 'You criticise your partner at your own expense'.

Playing with a pest

'Greenfly and black spot, that's what it is.'

The expert was making his annual inspection of my pathetic window boxes. 'Same everywhere I go, if it isn't mildew or leaf curl, it's . . .', he continued. My concentration wandered as he started a learned disclosure on systemic poisons.

How like a garden a bridge club is, I thought. Both have their pests. The names and faces of the bridge pest may differ, but they are to be found in any bridge club. I am sure you must have met Trigger Happy Henry or the Parrot.

Trigger Happy Henry is addicted to penalty doubles. It is no deterrent that his hand is totally unsuitable. So strong is the addiction, it never occurs to him that he would get better results by simply bidding his games. It might not be so bad if his shortcomings stopped there, but to make things worse he often assumes that your doubles are optional, and takes them out.

Here is a recent experience of one of Henry's dynamic doubles.

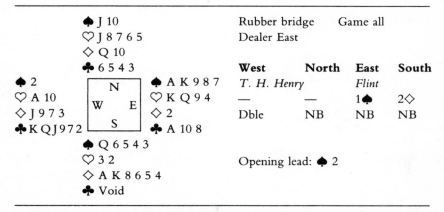

	♠ J 10		Rubber bridge	Game all		
	♡ J 8 7 6 5		Dealer East			
	◇ Q 10					
	♣ 6 5 4 3		**West**	**North**	**East**	**South**
♠ 2		♠ A K 9 8 7	T. H. Henry		Flint	
♡ A 10		♡ K Q 9 4	—	—	1♠	2◇
◇ J 9 7 3		◇ 2	Dble	NB	NB	NB
♣ K Q J 9 7 2		♣ A 10 8				
	♠ Q 6 5 4 3					
	♡ 3 2		Opening lead: ♠ 2			
	◇ A K 8 6 5 4					
	♣ Void					

Knowing Henry as I did, I should have firmly removed his double to two no trumps, although playing with any normal partner that would be an unforgivable bid.

After winning the opening lead with the ♠K, it was not difficult to form a picture of the hand as a whole. South's distribution was either 5-2-6-0 or 5-1-6-1. Prospects were poor. The best hope seemed to be to shorten declarer's trumps. So at trick two I played the ♣A. Not unexpectedly, South ruffed and continued with the ♠4.

With some relief, I calculated that declarer would either run short of trumps and therefore be unable to enjoy the ♠Q, or if he drew trumps, his final tally would be precisely seven tricks. I had reckoned without Henry. Nursing me, he ruffed the spade and continued with a club.

This inspired line of defence permitted declarer to make four club ruffs in his hand, two spade ruffs in dummy, which together with the ◇AK, made exactly eight tricks. As I painfully worked out that six clubs would have been unbeatable, Henry was busy piling Ossa on Pelion.

'If you play a trump at trick two, partner, we can get him down – when you didn't play a trump, I thought you didn't have one.' Poor Henry, there is no cure for him. The best you can do if you cut him is to remember his addiction.

The Parrot is seen in a rich variety of colours. His repetition may take the form of exaggerating his strength or weakness, over-emphasizing the shape he has already shown, or restating that his hand was unsuited to defence when it was already blatantly apparent. Here is a case in point:

	♠ 2	Rubber bridge		Love all
	♡ K Q 4	Dealer South		
	◇ A K Q J 9 8 7			
	♣ A K			

♠ K 4 3		♠ A J	**West**	**North**	**East**	**South**
♡ 3 2	N	♡ A J 10 9 8 7				*Parrot*
◇ 6 5	W E	◇ 3 2	—	—	—	3♠
♣ Q 9 8 7 6 4	S	♣ J 5 2	NB	3NT	NB	4♠
			NB	NB	NB	—

♠ Q 10 9 8 7 6 5	
♡ 6 5	
◇ 10 4	Opening lead: ♡3
♣ 10 3	

East took the ♡Q with the ♡A and returned the ♡J. The Parrot was in dummy and played a spade which East won with the ♠A, the Parrot flashily contributing the ♠10. East shrewdly switched to a diamond, which the Parrot won in hand. It was utterly predictable that he should 'guess' wrong, continuing with a small spade.

'Sorry, partner – had to take you out of three no trumps – my hand was utterly useless except in spades. I had eight of them', he lied.

'If I had continued with four no trumps over four spades', North asked gently, 'what would you have done?'

'Oh, I would have honoured your Blackwood.'

'Very frustrating hand,' said North. 'As the cards lie, we can make 10 tricks in no trumps. But apparently there was no way we could bid it.'

Timely Tactics

'Excuse me, Mr Dogberry, there's a telephone call for you.'

The interruption had come at a dramatic moment. Dogberry had just become the declarer in a contract of seven no trumps.

'Peter could play the hand for you', West offered.

The suggestion fell on deaf ears. Dogberry, who had suffered Peter's 'help' before, clutched his hand determinedly and hurried to the telephone.

'If I had to permit a substitute to play a hand for me' said the Club Expert, 'I would prefer to let him play a grand slam than a part score.'

The rest of the table greeted the disclosure with jeering disbelief. Before the expert had time to enlarge, Dogberry returned, his face wreathed in smiles.

'I'm terribly sorry, have to make this rubber only two more hands. Good news from the hospital', he explained.

The slam presented no difficulty and Dogberry claimed his contract. This was the penultimate deal of the rubber:

♠ A 2	North-South game		
♡ J 4 3	Dealer North		
◇ A K 10 4 2			
♣ A J 10			

			West	North	East	South
♠ K Q 8 7 6 5	N	♠ 3				*Dogberry*
♡ A Q 10	W E	♡ K 9 5	—	1◇	NB	1♡
◇ 8 7 6	S	◇ 9 5 3	1♠	2♡	NB	NB
♣ 5		♣ K 9 8 7 6 4	NB	—	—	—

♠ J 10 9 4
♡ 8 7 6 2
◇ Q J
♣ Q 3 2

Opening lead: ♠ K

'I might have underbid', said North as he put his hand on the table.

Dogberry, looking at the moth-eaten texture of his side's combined trump holding, decided to establish his side suit winners. He took the ♠K with the ♠A, returned to his hand with the ◇Q and finessed the ♣Q, which lost to East's ♣K.

The defence thoroughly enjoyed the next seven tricks. West ruffed the club return, cashed the ♠Q and continued with the ♠5, ruffed in dummy and over-ruffed by East. Nothing could prevent the defence from making their remaining four trumps separately at West ruffed clubs and East ruffed spades, making eight tricks.

'Only three down', said East. 'Lucky you underbid.'

Dogberry's mistake is common. Provided there is no great threat in a side suit, it is correct to play trumps, irrespective of the trump suit's anaemic quality. To understand the logic behind this, imagine that you are defending a contract where declarer's main source of tricks will come from a cross ruff. Everyone knows the right game for the defence is to play trumps at every opportunity.

Declarer must recognize the type of hand where the customary roles are reversed and trumps are no use to him. Because he wishes he was in no trumps, it follows that it is correct to 'draw trumps'. On this hand, if Dogberry had played trumps at every opportunity it would have made at least two, possibly three, tricks difference.

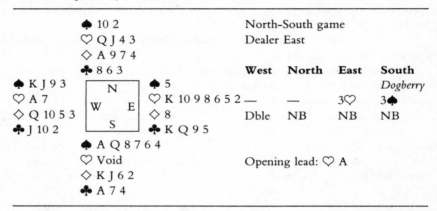

	♠ 10 2			North-South game			
	♡ Q J 4 3			Dealer East			
	◇ A 9 7 4						
	♣ 8 6 3						
♠ K J 9 3		♠ 5		**West**	**North**	**East**	**South**
♡ A 7	N	♡ K 10 9 8 6 5 2					*Dogberry*
◇ Q 10 5 3	W E	◇ 8		—	—	3♡	3♠
♣ J 10 2	S	♣ K Q 9 5		Dble	NB	NB	NB
	♠ A Q 8 7 6 4						
	♡ Void			Opening lead: ♡ A			
	◇ K J 6 2						
	♣ A 7 4						

Dogberry ruffed the ♡A, entered dummy with the ◇A, and finessed the ♠Q. The club expert switched to the ♣J, which Dogberry won with the ♣A. He tried the ♠A, on which East discarded a heart.

'I expect the diamonds are 4–1 as well', said Dogberry, who was a better prophet than a card player. The defence did not slip, defeating the contract by three tricks; 800 to East-West.

'How contrary you are', said North, 'on a hand where you should draw trumps you don't, and when you shouldn't you do.'

In fairness, this is the sort of hand which distinguishes the tyro from the average player, never mind the expert. Warned of the bad trump break, a good declarer would never tackle the trumps as Dogberry did. An expert would probably attempt to sever the defence's communications, and at the same time discover the exact distribution.

The play might develop like this: after ruffing the ♡A declarer plays a small club. East will win and switch to a trump which declarer finesses to West's ♠J. West will probably continue clubs. Declarer wins the ♣A and

plays a third round of clubs. This is the position after the first five tricks, of
which the defence have made three.

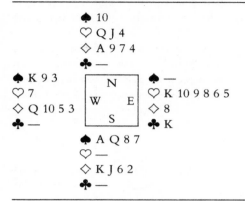

I have assumed that West has won the third round of clubs (nothing would
be gained by East overtaking). West plays a heart, dummy's ♡Q is
covered by East and ruffed by South, who now knows the exact
distribution. He will continue with the ◇K, noting East's ◇8, and follow
with the ◇J, covered by the ◇Q and taken by dummy's ◇A. Declarer
continues with a third round of diamonds, which West wins. West can
only exit with the fourth round of diamonds. When declarer plays the
♠10, West makes his ♠K to defeat the contract by one trick.

'Our grand slam didn't do us much good', said North, adding up the
score. 'When you were on the telephone we were discussing whether it
was easier to play a grand slam or a part score. What do you think,
Dogberry?'

But Dogberry had gone.

A loser every time

Oliver Overtrump is thought to be the oldest member; he is certainly the
club's greatest bore. Some years ago he gave up playing bridge to
concentrate on the infinitely more pleasurable occupation of watching the
mistakes and disasters of others. You can see him nearly every afternoon
lurking by the porter's desk waiting for an unwary victim.

'I would much appreciate your expert opinion on this hand,' he says as
he steers his prey to his favourite table in the coffee room. It is a fitting

tribute to the power of the old boy's tenacious grasp that this particular table is known as 'Colditz'.

This afternoon the unwilling audience was provided by a bright new young member. Overtrump had already launched on his hectoring prologue.

'Trouble with young players is they concentrate on technique at the expense of psychology; they're too inflexible. Look at this hand, for example.' And he produced a crumpled piece of paper from his pocket.

♠ A Q 10
♡ A J 7 6
◇ A J 5
♣ 8 6 2

```
      N
   W     E
      S
```

♠ J 9 6 4
♡ K Q 10 8 3
◇ Q 10 9
♣ A

Rubber bridge   North-South game
Dealer South

West	North	East	South
—	—	—	1♡
2♣	2◇	NB	3◇
NB	3♠	NB	4♠
NB	6♡	NB	NB
Dble	Redble	NB	NB
NB	—	—	—

Opening lead: ◇ 8

'South was a good player. North, as you can judge from his bidding, was capable of some imaginative strokes. West was no expert, but no fool either. How do you play the hand?'

The young man thought for a while.

'West probably has both the ◇K and the ♠K to justify his double, but why should I risk an unnecessary ruff? I win the ◇A, draw trumps, and rely on the spade finesse.'

'Exactly', Overtrump chortled, 'you completely failed to give West any justifiable motive for his double. These were the East-West hands', he continued, completing the diagram in his spidery scrawl.

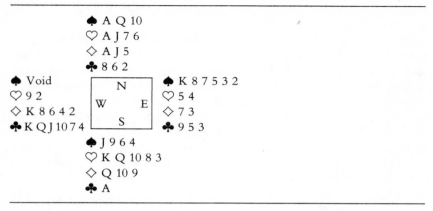

♠ A Q 10
♥ A J 7 6
♦ A J 5
♣ 8 6 2

♠ Void
♥ 9 2
♦ K 8 6 4 2
♣ K Q J 10 7 4

♠ K 8 7 5 3 2
♥ 5 4
♦ 7 3
♣ 9 5 3

♠ J 9 6 4
♥ K Q 10 8 3
♦ Q 10 9
♣ A

'Sensible players don't double slams to obtain an extra hundred. West, having heard diamonds bid and supported, hoped to give his partner a ruff. A spade return would establish a vicious defensive cross ruff. If you had reconsidered the bidding sequence, you might have recognized that the defence would expect your side to have more than six diamonds between you. As for your superficial analysis, if West were relying on his two kings, surely he would have preferred a passive club lead.'

The young man looked suitably crestfallen.

'Quite right, sir. Now if you'll excuse me, I must make a telephone call.'

'The machine is out of order.' Overtrump paused and produced another grimy scrap of paper.

'Now let's see if your technique is better than your psychology,' he said.

♠ A 5 4
♥ Q 10 3 2
♦ 10 4
♣ K Q 10 3

♠ K Q J 9 7 3
♥ A 6
♦ Q 8 7 3
♣ 5

Rubber bridge   East-West game
Dealer South

West	North	East	South
—	—	—	1♠
Dble	Redble	2♥	NB
4♥	Dble	NB	4♠
NB	NB	NB	—

Opening lead: ♦ A

'You may disapprove of South's bidding, but the only way to avoid North's anger is to make four spades. On the ♦A East plays the ♦9. West continues with the ◇K, on which East discards the ♡4. West persists with a third diamond. Now it's up to you.'

'You're right, sir, perhaps I am a better technician than a psychologist, because this seems fairly straightforward. I ruff the third diamond with the ♠A, draw trumps, cash the ◇Q and reduce the hand to a three card ending. To justify his four heart bid, West must hold the ♡K and the ♣A. He will be forced to unguard his ♡K or let me end-play him.'

'Ten out of ten for technique,' said Overtrump, 'but no marks for deduction. Who but a lunatic, at this vulnerability, having been warned by North's redouble, would jump to four hearts with only ♡Kxx. The only explanation must be exceptional distribution, in this case a spade void. Your admirable play would be stillborn, because as you failed to finesse the ♠9 at trick four, you would be unable to draw the trumps without East making his ♠10.'

The young man resolved to look round carefully when he entered the club in future.

Divide and rue

Horace Paradine is a perfectionist: worse, a mathematical perfectionist. His academic grasp of the game entitles him to some respect, but his pedantic and humourless impracticality ensures that he remains unpopular. There is one notable exception to the general view, Charles Grandace, the club expert. He is aware of Horace's shortcomings. But for him, at least, Horace's technical knowledge makes him an acceptable, if dangerous, partner, and because he is utterly predictable, he is the ideal opponent.

	♠ 8 7	
	♡ K J 5 4	
	◇ A K J 10 9	
	♣ 6 2	

♠ A J 4   N   ♠ 10 9 5 3 2
♡ Q 9 2   W   E   ♡ 3
◇ 8 2   S   ◇ Q 7 6
♣ K J 9 7 5   ♣ Q 8 4 3

	♠ K Q 6	
	♡ A 10 8 7 6	
	◇ 5 4 3	
	♣ A 10	

Rubber bridge   Game all
Dealer South

West	North	East	South
		Charles	*Horace*
—	—	—	1♡
NB	4♡	NB	NB
NB	—	—	—

Opening lead: ◇ 8

Horace thanked his partner gravely, and began to calculate the odds. After some minutes of loving attention to his moustache, he took the diamond with dummy's ◇K, and played a spade. West took the ♠A and switched to a club. Predictably, Horace misguessed the heart.

'That was a really unlucky hand', said Horace. 'The chance of losing no hearts is 52½ per cent. Of the remaining 47½ per cent, I would have succeeded half the time, whenever Charles has the Ace of spades. Even if one disregards the diamond finesse, I make that 76.25 per cent.'

Charles was smugly scribbling the hand down on a piece of paper, while making insincere clucking noises. Charles's interest in the hand owed nothing to Horace's mathematical dissertation, but to the recognition that provided the hearts are not 4-0 there is a line which guarantees the contract. Win the diamond in dummy with the ◇K, return to the ♡A and play a diamond. If West ruffs he is ruffing a loser. Whether West discards or follows, take the ◇A and play a third diamond. Dummy's ♡K provides an entry to discard the ♣10 on an established diamond.

After Charles and his partner won the rubber, they cut for partners.

'You and I, Horace,' said Charles, pretending to look pleased. They survived an unnecessary exercise at the five level to score the first game. Charles's delight when Horace opened two clubs on the next hand was no pretence. This was the full auction:

♠ 10 8 2	Rubber bridge	
♡ A J 4	North-South game	
◇ A 8 7 6	Dealer South	
♣ 9 4 2		

♠ Void	N	♠ Q 7 4 3
♡ Q 10 9 8 7 3 2	W E	♡ Void
◇ K Q 9	S	◇ J 10 5 4 3 2
♣ 10 8 7		♣ 6 5 3

♠ A K J 9 6 5
♡ K 6 5
◇ Void
♣ A K Q J

West	North	East	South
	Charles		Horace
—	—	—	2♣
NB	2NT	NB	3♠
NB	4♣	NB	6♣
NB	NB	NB	—

Opening lead: ◇ K

Horace discarded a heart on dummy's ◇A. He played a spade to his ♠K. The 4-0 trump break was a complication. Horace stared at the ceiling and eventually played a heart to dummy's ♡A, which East ruffed. East returned a diamond, and poor Horace could find no way to avoid a second trump loser.

'The chances of finding a suit divided 7-0 are only 0.5217 per cent. If one remembers East's failure to make a Lightner double, I think you will

71

agree, Charles, that the attempt to make an overtrick was mathematically sound'.

Charles was not amused.

'Even if the overtrick would have made the difference of a point, I most certainly would not agree. As it was, your purposeless folly was merely gilding the lily.'

'*Painting* the lily', corrected Horace, with no hint of contrition.

Beware, rabbits

Bridge can be an exasperating game. For a change you cut a good player against two rabbits. To your mortification, the rabbits, assisted by a generous slice of luck, run rings round you. A recent rubber of this sort reminded me of an old time expert's favourite aphorism. He would glower at each opponent in turn, and snort, 'Lovely bidding, lovely play'.

♠ K J
♡ A 10 4 2
◇ A 9 6
♣ A 10 4 3

Rubber bridge   Love all
Dealer West

West	North	East	South
NB	1NT	NB	2♣
NB	2♡	NB	5♠
NB	6♠	NB	NB
NB	—	—	—

♠ A 10 9 7 6 4
♡ K 3
◇ K 7 2
♣ K 2

Opening lead: ◇ Q

Declarer, one of the rabbits, won the trick with his ◇K and successfully finessed the ♠J. When the ♠Q fell on the next round of trumps, there was no further problem. As he wrote down the score, South turned to me.

'Do you approve of my bidding?' I said I did not.

There was a sequence which precisely described his hand. The bidding should have gone:

North	South
1 NT	3 ♠
3 NT	4 ♠

'As you have apparently overidden your partner's decision to play in no trumps', I went on, 'there can only be one logical explanation. You must hold a hand that is too strong to bid one no trump-four spades; in other words, a good hand with a moderate six-card suit. Partner is invited to bid the slam if his hand contains controls and a strong doubleton trump.'

'I'm so glad you *didn't* bid like that', North simpered. 'I would have passed four spades without giving the matter a second thought.'

South did not ask me my opinion of his play, which was equally misconceived. Superficially, it is an even money guess which way to finesse the spade. But if West has ♠Qxxx South has no chance. Whereas if East has the spade length, declarer can *normally still succeed by a trump reduction.*

	♠ A J 9 8 4 3	Rubber bridge	North-South game
	♡ A 10 2	Dealer South	
	◇ 10 7 6		
	♣ 6		

West	**North**	**East**	**South**
—	—	—	NB
NB	1♠	2♣	2♡
3♣	3♡	NB	4♡
NB	NB	NB	—

West:
♠ 2
♡ 9 5 4 3
◇ J 5 4 3
♣ K Q 7 4

East:
♠ K Q 5
♡ 8
◇ K 9 8 2
♣ A J 10 5 2

South:
♠ 10 7 6
♡ K Q J 7 6
◇ A Q
♣ 9 8 3

Opening lead: ♠ 2

I wish I could afford to pass hands as strong as South's.

Declarer took dummy's ♠A, cashed the ♡10 and played a second spade. West could see the danger of permitting East to hold the trick, but ruffing the spade and playing a trump would rely on East playing a foot-perfect defence. East decided that he must shorten dummy's trumps because if South had six hearts he would succeed by establishing the spades. So he played the ♣A and continued with another club. South recognized that he could not enjoy the long spades. However, if the King of diamonds was right, another club ruff would give him ten tricks.

After some puffing and blowing South scrambled home.

'Well played!' said North.

'Do you make the rubber 15?' South enquired.

Gloomily I reflected that if I had trumped the second spade, we would probably have defeated the contract. Then I realized that if declarer had played a club at trick two, there was no possible defence. 'Lovely bidding, lovely play' − and indifferent defence, I thought to myself with a smile.

Dogberry gets ruff treatment

Dogberry had been to a wedding. His demeanour suggested it, his clothes proved it. In his present mood, it would be hard to imagine a more unsuitable partner than Gerald Carp, whose acerbic tongue could make even strong men quail.

'Been to a wedding, I see', sniffed Carp.

'Yes, Richard Robinson's girl — quite enchanting . . .' Carp cut him short.

'It would be more expedient to consider the conventions of our marriage of convenience than recapture the lyrical moments of the other ceremony. I suggest a strong no trump throughout.'

The early skirmishes provided each side with a game, and Carp with some good opportunities for his destructive wit. Dogberry, totally unruffled, dealt at game all.

```
                ♠ A K J 8 4          Rubber bridge     Game all
                ♡ A K                Dealer South
                ◇ K 8
                ♣ Q J 10 2
  ♠ Void      ┌─────────┐  ♠ 10 9 7 6 3 2   West    North   East   South
  ♡ J 9 6 3   │    N    │  ♡ Q 5 2                   Carp           Dog-
  ◇ Q 10 7 5 3│ W     E │  ◇ J 9 4                                  berry
  ♣ 9 7 4 3   │    S    │  ♣ 8         —      —       —      1♣
              └─────────┘               NB     2♠      NB     2NT
                ♠ Q 5                    NB     4NT     NB     5♡
                ♡ 10 8 7 4               NB     5NT     NB     6◇
                ◇ A 6 2                  NB     7♣      NB     NB
                ♣ A K 6 5                NB     —       —      —
```

Opening lead: ♣ 3

'Possibly imprudent of me to put you into a grand slam in your present — er — effervescent condition', said Carp as he displayed his handsome dummy.

'Don't worry, Carp old thing, Doggers is up to this one.'

Dogberry allowed the lead to run up to his hand, winning the trick with the ♣K. A club to dummy revealed the 4-1 break. Dogberry continued with the King and Ace of diamonds, and ruffed the ◇6 in dummy. He cashed dummy's ♣Q and then played a spade to his ♠Q. West ruffed.

'Would you believe it?' said Dogberry. 'Clubs 4-1 and spades 6-0. You must admit that was unlucky.'

'I do not', said Carp. 'If you had taken the elementary precaution of winning the first two rounds of trumps in dummy, after taking the diamond ruff you would have been able to return your hand by overtaking dummy's last club, avoiding the unnecessary hazard of the spade ruff. How wonderful it must be to sprinkle your money as if it were confetti.'

'I'm dreadfully sorry', said Dogberry, suitably penitent. 'What is worse, I have sprinkled *your* money like confetti, which is something I am sure you would never do yourself.'

No dispensation for duffers

Gerald Carp, who had cut the Ace of spades, noted with pleasure that the club expert had drawn the Ace of diamonds. His pleasure was short-lived.

'You and I, Carp' said Eustace, the duffer of duffers, brandishing the Ace of hearts.

'I'll stay here', said Carp gruffly.

'The red cards have won the last four rubbers', Eustace suggested brightly. 'What's more, they were responsible for bringing us together'.

'I'll take the blue', said Carp.

♠ A Q		Rubber bridge	Love all
♡ 6 5 4		Dealer East	
◇ A 5 3			
♣ 10 9 8 7 6			

	West	North	East	South
				Club
	Eustace		*Carp*	*Expert*
	—	—	1♣	1♠
	2♡	2♣	NB	NB
	NB	—	—	—

West hand: ♠ 10 6 5 ♡ A Q J 10 7 ◇ 6 4 2 ♣ 4 2

East hand: ♠ K 3 2 ♡ K 9 ◇ 10 9 7 ♣ A Q J 5 3

South hand: ♠ J 9 8 7 4 ♡ 8 3 2 ◇ K Q J 8 ♣ K

Opening lead: ♣ 4

Carp took the first trick with the ♣A and switched to the ♡K. Eustace brightly overtook the ♡K with the ♡A and cashed two more hearts, Carp discarding the ◇7. Obediently, as he thought, Eustace switched to a diamond, which declarer won in hand. Although the spade finesse lost, the defence could take no more tricks. If Eustace had played a club, the defence could have promoted the ♠10 for the setting trick.

'Looked like a high diamond to me', said Eustace, smarting under Carp's withering scorn. But Carp was the real culprit. He should have ruffed the third heart and played a club himself.

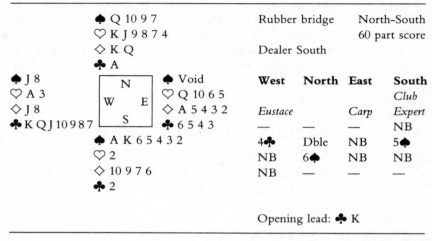

♠ Q 10 9 7
♡ K J 9 8 7 4
♢ K Q
♣ A

♠ J 8
♡ A 3
♢ J 8
♣ K Q J 10 9 8 7

♠ Void
♡ Q 10 6 5
♢ A 5 4 3 2
♣ 6 5 4 3

♠ A K 6 5 4 3 2
♡ 2
♢ 10 9 7 6
♣ 2

Rubber bridge   North-South
                 60 part score

Dealer South

West	North	East	South
			Club
Eustace		*Carp*	*Expert*
—	—	—	NB
4♣	Dble	NB	5♠
NB	6♠	NB	NB
NB	—	—	—

Opening lead: ♣ K

South took the club with dummy's ace and returned to hand with the ♠K, on which Carp discarded the ♢5. When South continued with a low heart, Eustace 'put him to a guess' by playing low. Declarer needed no further assistance.

'Didn't you see my ♢5?' raged Carp. 'Did you suppose that South would pass originally with seven spades to the AK and the ♢A?'

'Looked like a small diamond to me', said Eustace meekly.

The club expert could not help feeling sorry for poor Eustace. 'If you had discarded the ♡Q, Carp, you would doubtless have prevented the accident.'

While Carp blustered, an emboldened Eustace impertinently agreed. 'Yes, why didn't you?'

The boring wizard of odds

Horace Paradine, the mathematical bore, and the querulous Gerald Carp disliked each other intensely. Neither man took any pains to conceal his aversion.

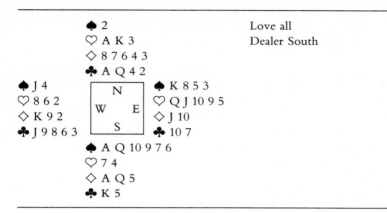

♠ 2
♡ A K 3
◇ 8 7 6 4 3
♣ A Q 4 2

Love all
Dealer South

♠ J 4
♡ 8 6 2
◇ K 9 2
♣ J 9 8 6 3

♠ K 8 5 3
♡ Q J 10 9 5
◇ J 10
♣ 10 7

♠ A Q 10 9 7 6
♡ 7 4
◇ A Q 5
♣ K 5

Paradine, South, playing in the ambitious contract of six spades, received the lead of the ♡8, which he won with dummy's ♡K. He played a trump to his ♠Q and continued with the ♠A and ♠10, which Carp, sitting East won with the ♠K. When Carp switched to the ◇J, Paradine rejected the finesse and played out his three remaining trumps, discarding diamonds from dummy. When declarer cashed his ♡A West was unable to keep both the ◇K and his guard in clubs.

'Well played', said one of the spectators.

'Good guess in spades', said another.

'Guess!' sniffed Paradine, as if he had been accused of some outrageous solecism. 'I leave guessing to my inspired friend Gerald here. If the spades break three-three, there's nothing in it, I grant you, but when they divide four-two, the play of the Queen gains against Jx in the West hand. If West has Kx, you can't help losing two trump tricks.'

'As for the ending', Paradine droned on, 'the lead and the early play revealed that East had nine cards in the majors, so mathematically West may be assumed to have the length and strength in the minors.'

Carp seethed inwardly, but recognized that anything he might say would smack of sour grapes. 'Revenge is a dish best eaten cold', he thought, and wrote RIADBEC on his score pad to remind him to keep his temper.

'You're not allowed to write down your conventions', said Paradine sternly.

'It is only a note to ring a Hungarian friend of mine', replied Carp smoothly.

Paradine studied the next hand (set out overleaf) carefully before winning the lead with his ♡K. He crossed to dummy's ◇A, and ruffed a diamond. A club was won by West with the ♣J. West persevered with a second

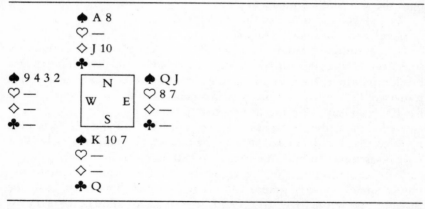

	♠ A 8		North-South game			
	♡ A 6 5		Dealer North			
	◇ A J 10 8 6					
	♣ 10 4 3					
			West	**North**	**East**	**South**
♠ 9 4 3 2		♠ Q J			*Carp*	*Paradine*
♡ Q 9		♡ J 8 7 3 2	—	1NT	NB	2♠
◇ K 5 4 3		◇ Q 9 2	NB	NB	NB	—
♣ A J 7		♣ K 9 6				
	♠ K 10 7 6 5					
	♡ K 10 4		Opening lead: ♡ Q			
	◇ 7					
	♣ Q 8 5 2					

heart. Paradine won with dummy's Ace, and ruffed another diamond.
When Paradine played another club, West allowed Carp to win the trick
with the ♣K. Carp cashed the ♡J, West discarding the ◇K, and then put
West on play with the ♣A.

This was the four-card ending with West on play. Paradine had made
five tricks, and required three of the last four to make his contract.

	♠ A 8	
	♡ —	
	◇ J 10	
	♣ —	
♠ 9 4 3 2		♠ Q J
♡ —		♡ 8 7
◇ —		◇ —
♣ —		♣ —
	♠ K 10 7	
	♡ —	
	◇ —	
	♣ Q	

West perforce continued with the ♠2 to North's ♠8, Carp's ♠Q, and
Paradine's ♠K. West ruffed the ♣Q with his ♠3, dummy overruffed
with the ♠A, while Carp discarded a heart. On the ◇J Carp discarded his
last heart, and, in deference to the odds, Paradine trumped with the ♠7,
losing to West's ♠9. One down.

'Horace, you're a magician. The way you managed to make only two
trump tricks with A 8 in dummy and K 10 7 in your hand when I had the
Q J alone was pure wizardry.'

FOUR

Great battles from the past

How good a bridge player was Culbertson? Great showman though he was, he was certainly a most difficult partner. Contemporaries say that his wife Josephine was a more effective player. But his innumerable boasts were largely fulfilled in America, and it was only when he came to Europe that the Austrians put him firmly in his place.

Many of the giants have died, some no longer play. But even today bridge players are still influenced by Culbertson's early theories, by Lightner's slam double, and Jacoby's transfers, to mention but a few. Ten years from now, however well the stars of the 1990s may play, I feel sure that bridge players will look back with admiration at the wonderful play of the Blue team and the determination of the American Aces.

Replaying old battles

When cricket lovers meet, a frequent topic of discussion is the comparative merits of players of different generations. Although it can only be a matter of opinion whether Hutton's application or Bradman's cavalier dominance match the professionalism of Boycott and Chappell, it does not subtract from the animation of the debate. With athletics it is a different story. Sadly we must accept the evidence of the stop watch that Roger Bannister would trail yards behind Coe and Ovett.

The accuracy of a similar comparison of bridge players falls between these two extremes, because the records of old matches provide some degree of proof. My own impression is that the standard of dummy play improved sharply between 1930 and the mid-1950s but has made little progress since then.

The defence of the top players gets better all the time, but it is the bidding that would provoke the most controversy. It is demonstrable that Colonel Beasley's methods would be as effective as a bow and arrow in today's bridge battles, but some of Culbertson's ideas form the basis of modern bidding.

The success of the Italian Blue team in the late 1950s induced a swing to One Club systems. In the last few years the fashion has started to switch back. In theory, One Club systems are more accurate; in practice they suffer from two defects. It used to be the universal custom to listen politely while the Italian maestros conducted their duet. No longer. Modern players appreciate that aggressive intervention pays handsome dividends.

The strong One Club is a two-edged sword. It proclaims a strong hand, but gives no indication of the type of strong hand; nor does it give any clue about which suit or suits form the strength. If the defending side can put up a barrage balloon, the One Club bidder is forced to display his wares at an uncomfortably high level.

The second objection to strong One Club systems is a human one. Many of the more complicated sequences are pearls of rare beauty. They remain locked away in the cupboard of a player's memory for years at a time. All too frequently, when the cupboard is opened, the memory has become dusty even if the pearls have not.

Culbertson's incessant boasting eventually provoked Hal Sims and his wife Dorothy to accept the challenge to a match of 150 rubbers which started on 25 March 1932, in New York. Culbertson's suave appearance was a transparent mask for the aggressive, calculating, if brilliant showman that he really was. If he was conceited before his victory over his old rival Sidney Lenz, now he had become insufferable. The bidding on this hand reveals some primitive notions, but it was during the play that the hubbub arose.

	♠ Q J 7			Game all			
	♡ J 5 4 3			Dealer West			
	◇ 9						
	♣ A K 10 5 2			West	North	East	South
♠ A		N	♠ 10 9 6 4 3	Sims	Mrs	Mrs	Culbert-
♡ 10 8 6 2	W		E	♡ 7		Culbertson	Sims	son
◇ K Q J 8 6		S	◇ 7 5 3 2	NB	NB	NB	1♡
♣ J 9 7			♣ Q 6 2	NB	2♣	NB	2♠
	♠ K 8 5 2			NB	5♡	NB	NB
	♡ A K Q 9			NB	—	—	—
	◇ A 10 4						
	♣ 8 4			Opening lead: ◇ K			

Although Culbertson's choice of opening bid would receive the endorsement of modern experts, the reason for his selection most certainly would not. Apparently his intention was to make a show of strength with a reverse rebid of two spades. Whereas a reverse should show strength, it should also promise at least five cards in his first bid suit, hearts. Josephine Culbertson's bidding was even stranger. The response of two clubs by a passed hand is non-forcing by modern standards. A jump to three clubs is used to describe a hand which contains a fit for partner's suit and is near to maximum for an initial pass. Her bid of five hearts, produced after an agonized trance, was an overstatement.

Culbertson won the opening lead with the ◇A and cashed the ♡A and ♡K. He followed with a spade which Sims won with the ♠A. Sims continued with the ◇Q, which Culbertson ruffed in dummy. At this point Culbertson paused for a considerable time. Eventually Mrs Sims jocularly inquired what he was thinking about.

'Whether I am going one down or two down', Culbertson replied lightly.

When Culbertson continued with dummy's ♠Q, Sims ruffed and persisted with a diamond which was ruffed in dummy. Because the clubs were divided 3-3, Culbertson was able to establish them, draw Sims' remaining trump and re-enter dummy with the ♠J.

As Sims was quick to notice, if instead of ruffing the ♠Q, he had discarded a club, the contract could have been defeated. If Culbertson continued with the ♠J, Sims could ruff and, by forcing dummy to ruff, promote a further trump trick for himself. He protested that his play had

81

been influenced by Culbertson's remark. But the protest was rejected by the match referee.

Still in New York, we turn the clock on 23 years to January, 1955, the only occasion on which Great Britain won the World Championship. The Americans had enjoyed absolute supremacy and even though some famous names were missing from their team in 1955, it was a fine victory by the British players.

This was Hand 33, played when Great Britain was leading, but by a margin which was far from decisive.

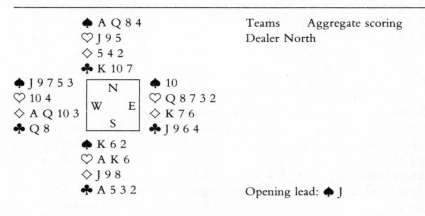

♠ A Q 8 4
♡ J 9 5
◇ 5 4 2
♣ K 10 7

♠ J 9 7 5 3   ♠ 10
♡ 10 4   ♡ Q 8 7 3 2
◇ A Q 10 3   ◇ K 7 6
♣ Q 8   ♣ J 9 6 4

♠ K 6 2
♡ A K 6
◇ J 9 8
♣ A 5 3 2

Teams   Aggregate scoring
Dealer North

Opening lead: ♠ J

The contract was the same in both rooms, three no trumps by South. Both Wests led the ♠J. In the open room the American declarer won the lead in dummy and ducked a club to West. As he could only enjoy three spade tricks, even the friendly switch to the ♡10 did not help. One down, 50 to Great Britain.

In the closed room, the British declarer was Adam Meredith. His bidding may have been unorthodox, but no one could have been a better card player. Meredith won the lead with the ♠K, and led the ◇J! This is a well-known subterfuge today. In 1955, it was a novelty.

The idea is to conceal one's weakness in the hope that the defence will make a disastrous switch. West won and continued with the ♠9. Meredith won with dummy's ♠Q. Notice that he now had four spade tricks but only eight tricks in all. Meredith played a second diamond, and when the defence persisted with a third spade, he played a third round of diamonds.

West could have cashed his thirteenth diamond, but correctly refrained from doing so as it would have squeezed his partner. He did his best by plodding on with a fourth spade. Declarer returned to his hand with the ♡K and ducked a club to East. East had already been forced to part with three hearts, and when he returned a club Meredith was able to read the distribution exactly, to drop the ♡Q.

No wonder all the experts called Meredith 'Plum'.

Pipped by the French

When I played in the sixth World Bridge Olympiad in 1980 in Valkenberg, Holland, it was natural if poignant for me to look back on the first Olympiad which was held in Turin in 1960.

Twenty-nine teams took part, and although both Britain and France could be considered live contenders, most neutral observers felt that the issue lay between Italy and America. America, as provided by the curious international rules in force at that time, was represented by no less than four different teams. Three qualified for the final rounds together with France, Great Britain and Italy.

In the finals, the early play established the pattern. The strongest American team never showed their true form, losing heavily to France and Britain. The Italians were defeated by Britain in a close match of high quality. Without the encouragement and inspiration of Perroux, the captain who had led them to three world championships, Italy seemed to lack resilience and lose heart.

So it was that with one round to go, only France or Britain could win the title. These two teams were level on victory points, but should both win their final match by a clear margin, Britain would be the winners.

In the final round France played Italy. Our opponents were an American team which had begun poorly. I, a raw young hopeful in those days, played the first session with Ralph Swimer in the closed room. Reese and Schapiro played in the open room. At the interval, we led by 25 IMPs and France led Italy by nine. You could not name the odds in our favour. Journalists anxious to get their copy off in time insisted on taking photographs of the British teams, giving credence to the superstition that such anticipation brings bad luck. For the second session the British captain very reasonably decided to rely on his front line troops, restoring Gardener and Rose to replace Swimer and me.

But now things began to go wrong for us. After the second session our lead had been reduced to 13 IMPs. Worse France was thrashing the demoralized Italians. The end is history. We lost the Olympiad by one victory point.

Twenty years have passed but Britain has never come so close again.

Here are two hands from the second session which show how easily the points can slip away, even when the position appears impregnable.

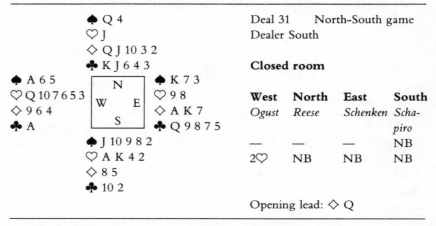

```
                ♠ Q 4
                ♡ J
                ◇ Q J 10 3 2
                ♣ K J 6 4 3
♠ A 6 5                          ♠ K 7 3
♡ Q 10 7 6 5 3    N              ♡ 9 8
◇ 9 6 4         W     E          ◇ A K 7
♣ A                S             ♣ Q 9 8 7 5
                ♠ J 10 9 8 2
                ♡ A K 4 2
                ◇ 8 5
                ♣ 10 2
```

Deal 31   North-South game
Dealer South

Closed room

West	North	East	South
Ogust	Reese	Schenken	Scha-piro
—	—	—	NB
2♡	NB	NB	NB

Opening lead: ◇ Q

In the closed room Ogust opened with a weak two bid. Notice Schenken's sound valuation of his hand, which permitted West to play in a comfortable part score. Nine tricks were made: 140 to East-West.

Open room

West	North	East	South
Gardener	Mathe	Rose	Allinger
—	—	—	NB
1 ♡	2 ◇	3 ♣	NB
3 ♡	NB	3 NT	Dble
NB	NB	NB	—

Opening lead: ◇ 8

In the open room Gardener's opening bid of one heart cannot be criticized. To pass, playing Acol, would be unthinkable. But I feel that Rose should have bid four hearts instead of three no trumps. Certainly it would have been wrong for Gardener to retire to four hearts. He had given an adequate description of his hand, now he had to respect his partner's judgement. In the play, Rose made the correct percentage play of finessing the ♡9. When this lost to North's ♡J, the hand collapsed. Six tricks were made: 500 to North-South.

The second hand contains some unusual points.

84

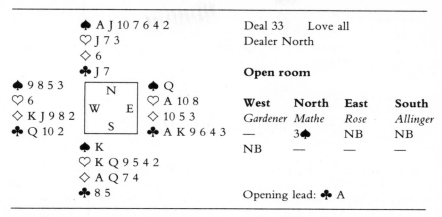

♠ A J 10 7 6 4 2
♡ J 7 3
♢ 6
♣ J 7

♠ 9 8 5 3
♡ 6
♢ K J 9 8 2
♣ Q 10 2

♠ Q
♡ A 10 8
♢ 10 5 3
♣ A K 9 6 4 3

♠ K
♡ K Q 9 5 4 2
♢ A Q 7 4
♣ 8 5

Deal 33   Love all
Dealer North

Open room

West	North	East	South
Gardener	Mathe	Rose	Allinger
—	3♠	NB	NB
NB	—	—	—

Opening lead: ♣ A

In the open room, ten tricks were made: 170 to North-South. An inspired defence could have defeated three spades. If East had switched to the ♡A before cashing the ♣K, he could have given West two heart ruffs.

Closed room

West	North	East	South
Ogust	Reese	Schenken	Schapiro
—	1♠	2♣	2♡
NB	2♠	NB	4♡
NB	NB	NB	—

Opening lead: ♣ 2

In the closed room, Reese tried a semi-psychic one spade opening which Schapiro followed with a good example of his preference for direct rather than exploratory bidding.

East cashed two clubs and continued with the ♠Q. Nine tricks were made: 50 to East-West.

The official account of the play tersely observes that the switch to the ♠Q effectively cut the communications. This analysis is false. Suppose that declarer overtakes the ♠K with dummy's Ace and continues with the ♠J, what can East do? If he ruffs, Schapiro can over-ruff and continue with the Ace and another diamond, ruffing in dummy. The continuation of the ♠10 would present East with an insoluble problem.

In describing these two hands I have presented an unflattering picture of the British players. One must remember that the first World Olympiad was an unprecedented test of stamina and concentration. Reese, Schapiro,

Gardener and Rose, as the leading two pairs, had been required to play considerably more than their fair share of the boards. It was only because of the consistent quality of their play that Britain had come so near to a memorable victory.

Death of the Blues

When Charles Goren and his American team-mates sat down to play the seventh world championship for the Bermuda Bowl in 1957, they were doubtless supremely confident. Only a few years before, their compatriots had comprehensively defeated an Italian team which included some of the same players who were in New York on this occasion. The Americans were in for a rude shock. Not only did they lose, but by the staggering margin of 10,150 points. The era of American dominance was over.

Incredible as it seems today, some critics dismissed the result as a fluke. But the Italian Blue team won ten successive Bermuda Bowls and the World Olympiads in 1964 and 1968. After a brief retirement, they returned to annex three more world championships and the Olympic title in 1972. From 1957 to 1975, they not only appeared invincible, they *were*.

Astonishingly, it is now several years since Italy won the championship. 1976 was the year when everything went awry. The narrow loss of the Olympiad was disappointing, but far less bitter than the defeat, in the final of the Bermuda Bowl, by the Americans. In 1977 they lost the European championship, and in 1979, despite a remarkable rally in the last 16 boards, they lost the Bermuda Bowl to the Americans again. The last few years have underlined the downward drift. Failure to qualify for the finals in Valkenburg in 1980 was followed by a dismal sixth place in the 1981 European championships.

What went wrong? There are, I believe, a number of reasons which have contributed to these poor results. It was in 1976 that an Italian player, who had failed to qualify for the team, accused some of the Italian players of using illegal signals. The Italians were accustomed to unjustified suspicion from jealous rivals, but this accusation by their own countryman was infinitely more damaging. It was surely no coincidence that their performance that year was by their high standards comparatively poor.

Carl Alberto Perroux's influence was a major factor in the Blue team's early successes. As a captain, he was a stern disciplinarian, who nevertheless inspired his men with a remarkable team spirit. He repeatedly demonstrated that he placed an equal reliance on each of his three pairs. Because they were overshadowed by the dazzling combination of Garozzo-Forquet and Avarelli-Belladonna, it is easy to underestimate the invaluable role that D'Alelio and Pabis Tici played. Neither they nor Avarelli have represented Italy since 1969. Forquet retired from the international scene in 1976, and the great Belladonna announced that 1979 was his last world championship.

Of the legendary Blue team, only Garozzo remains. Today, even he has his detractors, who dub him a 'Bridge Narcissus', implying that he has fallen in love with his own system. Someone cattily compared the Garozzo-Franco partnership in the 1981 European championship with two coloratura sopranos desperately trying to outshine each other.

The successful defence on this hand was by no means easy, but I feel that the Blue team in their prime would not have lost their way.

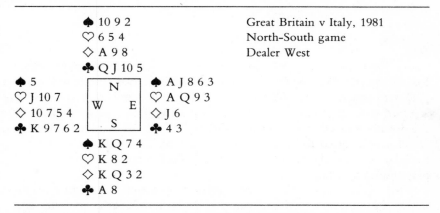

```
              ♠ 10 9 2                 Great Britain v Italy, 1981
              ♡ 6 5 4                  North-South game
              ◇ A 9 8                  Dealer West
              ♣ Q J 10 5
  ♠ 5            ┌─────────┐   ♠ A J 8 6 3
  ♡ J 10 7       │    N    │   ♡ A Q 9 3
  ◇ 10 7 5 4   W │       E │ E ◇ J 6
  ♣ K 9 7 6 2    │    S    │   ♣ 4 3
                 └─────────┘
              ♠ K Q 7 4
              ♡ K 8 2
              ◇ K Q 3 2
              ♣ A 8
```

In the closed room, Lauria played in three no trumps, as North. He received the lead of a low spade on which he unwisely contributed dummy's ♠K. He continued with the Ace and another club, losing to West's ♣K. West, Paul Hackett, had no difficulty finding the killing heart switch. One down, 100 to Great Britain.

This was the bidding in the open room:

West	North	East	South
Franco	*Sheehan*	*Garozzo*	*Rose*
NB	NB	1 ♠	1 NT
NB	2 ♣	NB	2 NT
NB	3 NT	NB	NB
NB	—	—	—

Opening lead: ♣ 2

Rose won the lead in dummy and played the ♠10, which Garozzo won with the ♠A. Garozzo correctly switched to the ♡3, which ran to Franco's ♡10. Franco continued with the ♡J. Rose took the ♡K and played two rounds of diamonds, ending in dummy. When the ♠9 was played, Garozzo was forced to cover with ♠J. This was the ending:

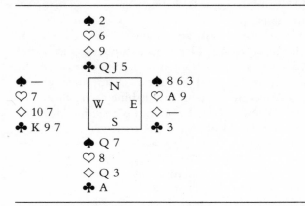

♠ 2
♡ 6
♢ 9
♣ Q J 5

♠ —
♡ 7
♢ 10 7
♣ K 9 7

N
W   E
S

♠ 8 6 3
♡ A 9
♢ —
♣ 3

♠ Q 7
♡ 8
♢ Q 3
♣ A

Rose cashed the ♣A and the ♢Q, East discarding a spade, and put East on play with a heart. East could cash his winning heart, but had to concede the last two tricks to declarer's ♠Q7. Good play by declarer admittedly, but the defence missed two chances. Although it is hard to judge, Garozzo could have averted the end play by taking the ♡A and playing a third round of the suit. If Franco had returned the ♡7, retaining the ♡J, the end play would also fail.

What of the future? Will Italy rise again? Few would dispute that young Italian players have the talent, even if they appear to lack the discipline and maturity of the Blue team. But give them the leadership of a great captain like Perroux, and I believe they might fulfil their undoubted potential.

Winning women

Most informed commentators predicted that the ladies series in the 6th World Bridge Olympiad in Valkenberg, 1980, would be won by the United States, Italy or Great Britain. They were right. With two rounds remaining, the United States and Italy were 27 VPs clear of the rest of the field, and in the run to the line, the former's greater experience proved decisive. The surprise, when you study the galaxy of stars at their disposal, is that this was the United States' first victory in the event. Mary Jane Farrell and Marilyn Johnson, Dorothy Truscott and Emma Jane Hawes, Jacqui Mitchell and Gail Moss are a strong, well-balanced team who thoroughly deserved their over-due success.

The British women started well, but defeats by France and Japan seemed to upset their rhythm. At one stage all hopes of a medal had apparently vanished. Then in the last few days they recovered their true form, scoring a string of impressive victories to finish strongly in third.

There is no doubt that the standard of women's bridge has improved considerably, and continues to do so. If for the moment men are better, in which particular department does their superiority lie? Depth – and before I am accused of smug chauvinism let me protest that it was a woman international who advanced this theory.

This is what she meant: sometimes a player will be faced with a critical decision towards the end of the play. Before making up their minds, great players will go back over the bidding and the play to make certain that there are no inferences, positive or negative, inconsistent with the assessment that they have made. They will also check that the picture they have formed of the distribution and location of the opposing high cards can be reconciled with their opponents' play. You may say that is not very difficult. Perhaps not on any given hand, but on each and every hand it requires unwavering concentration.

On this hand from the ladies series match between Denmark and Ireland, no man could improve on the play of the Danish declarer, Trine Dahl.

♠ 7 5 2		Board 8	North-South game	
♡ J		Dealer West		
◇ A Q 10 9 5				
♣ J 10 6 4				

			West	North	East	South
♠ Q 9 6 3	N	♠ J		Dorthe		Trine
♡ 6 5 4 3	W　E	♡ 10 9 8 2		Schaltz		Dahl
◇ 7 4 2	S	◇ 8 6 3	NB	NB	NB	1♠
♣ A K		♣ 9 8 7 5 2	NB	2♣	NB	4♠
♠ A K 10 8 4			NB	NB	NB	—
♡ A K Q 7						
◇ K J						
♣ Q 3			Opening lead: ♣ K			

West had given no hints in the bidding and her final pass was made without the slightest hesitation. West cashed the ♣A and switched to the ◇7. Declarer won in hand, and cashed the ♠K, on which East contributed the ♠J. Although the ♠J could have been a false card, South decided to accept it at face value. Recognizing that the probability of the ♠QJ is less than the singleton ♠J, she played on that basis. She crossed to dummy with the ♡J, cashed the ♢A and ruffed a diamond with the ♣4. She took two top hearts, but ruffed the ♡Q in dummy. Now when she played a spade from dummy and East showed out, she could play low, end-playing West in trumps.

Nicola Gardener is one of the stars of the British team. Although still in her thirties, she is already an experienced international and an automatic choice for any British team. She runs the London School of Bridge and writes a bridge column for a magazine. When I asked her for a hand on which she had shone she replied with becoming modesty that she could not remember one. Here is a hand that I remember well where the Bridgerama audience fully appreciated her incisive defence. It arose in the semi-finals of the Indian Nationals when Nicola was playing with an unfamiliar partner, India's outstanding player Rubi Roy.

♠ 6 3		
♡ J 9 8 7 4		
♢ K		
♣ A K 10 9 8		

♠ 2	N	♠ A K Q 8 7 4
♡ K 10 6	W E	♡ Q 5 2
♢ J 10 9 4 3	S	♢ 7 2
♣ Q 7 5 3		♣ 6 4

♠ J 10 9 5		
♡ A 3		
♢ A Q 8 6 5		
♣ J 2		

Teams   North-South game
Dealer West

West	North	East	South
Rubi Roy		*Nicola*	
		Gardener	
NB	1♡	2♠	3NT
NB	NB	NB	—

Opening lead: ♠ 2

North-South cannot be accused of underbidding, but with the club finesse right, there are nine tricks. Nicola took the ♠Q and paused to consider how she could disrupt declarer's communications. When you see all four hands it is not difficult to find the heart switch. It is a very different thing at the table. Declarer ducked, and Rubi Roy unerringly continued with another heart. No matter how he wriggled, declarer could only make eight tricks. With the ♡A removed, after he had taken dummy's five club tricks, he had no re-entry to his hand to enjoy the ♢AQ.

'That Nicola, she plays the cards very well', Rubi Roy confided to me after the session. 'If only she would learn my bidding system.'

It seemed tactful to convey Nicola's considerable respect for Rubi Roy's play without mentioning her comments on *his* bidding.

UK newcomers face a test of mettle

The British Bridge League has selected the following team to represent Britain in the European Championships in July (1983): G.T. Kirby – J.M. Armstrong; G. Duckworth – D.G. Price; A.H. Duncan – B.D. Short.

The results of the final trial which took place in Birmingham in January were:

1=. G.T.Kirby, J.M. Armstrong, A.H Duncan, B.D. Short, 43 VPs.
1=. G. Duckworth, D.G. Price, J.L. Reardon, R.J.A. Butland, 43 VPs.
3. R.M. Sheehan, W. Coyle, B. Shenkin, J. Flint, 19 VPs.
4. A.R. Forrester, R. Brock, S. Ray, B. Senior, 10 VPs.

The UK team contains some new faces. Kirby and Armstrong played for Britain in Lausanne in 1979, but the others will be making their début. Many will feel that Reardon and Butland, who played with commendable consistency, were especially unlucky to be overlooked, bearing in mind that their team had finished second in the earlier trial.

How should one interpret that unexpected result? Have the talented young players, who have waited patiently in the wings, finally claimed their rightful inheritance, or was the old guard's poor performance no more significant than Liverpool losing a match at home? We must wait and see.

Our match against the Kirby team produced a curious coincidence.

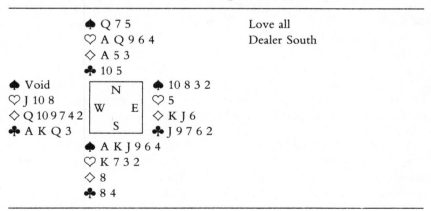

In the closed room our team mates, Coyle and Shenkin, bid five hearts which West (Short) doubled. Duncan led a club which Short took with the Queen. He then had to underplay his Ace and King of clubs to obtain a spade ruff for the setting trick. 100 to Kirby.

This was the bidding in the open room:

West	North	East	South
Flint	*Kirby*	*Sheehan*	*Armstrong*
—	—	—	1 ♠
2 ◇	2 ♡	NB	4 ♡
4 NT[1]	5 ♡	6 ♣	6 ♡
Double	NB	NB	NB

1 Usually six diamonds and four clubs.

After proper deliberation, Sheehan led the ◇K. Declarer won with the ◇A and ruffed a diamond in dummy. He drew trumps and claimed 13 tricks. Six hearts doubled, made with an overtrick, added up to 1,310 to Kirby, and a swing of 16 IMPs.

This was board 38 of the same match:

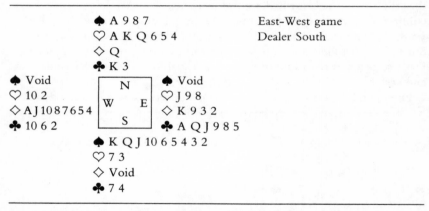

```
            ♠ A 9 8 7              East-West game
            ♡ A K Q 6 5 4         Dealer South
            ◇ Q
            ♣ K 3
 ♠ Void          N         ♠ Void
 ♡ 10 2                    ♡ J 9 8
 ◇ A J 10 8 7 6 5 4  W  E  ◇ K 9 3 2
 ♣ 10 6 2          S      ♣ A Q J 9 8 5
            ♠ K Q J 10 6 5 4 3 2
            ♡ 7 3
            ◇ Void
            ♣ 7 4
```

Coyle and Shenkin played in four spades, making 13 tricks. 510 to Sheehan.

The excitement was reserved for our room.

West	North	East	South
Sheehan	*Duncan*	*Flint*	*Short*
—	—	—	4 ♠
NB	4 NT	Double[1]	6 ♠
Double	NB	NB	NB

1 An unrehearsed attempt to attract a minor suit lead.

Sheehan led the ♢A. Short ruffed, drew a round of trumps to make certain that there were no lurkers, and claimed 13 tricks.

'Why did you double four no trumps?' Sheehan inquired.

'To get you to lead a minor', I replied.

'Well I led one, didn't I?' said Sheehan.

'How much does that score?' asked Short, naturally elated.

'1,310', said Sheehan.

'That was quick', said Duncan, 'you must be a mathematical wizard.'

'It's practice', said Sheehan sadly.

The rare Albatross

The Sixth World Team Olympiad 1980 attracted a record entry in both the open and ladies series, including several countries new to international competition. Inevitably, I suppose, politics made an unwelcome intrusion. In response to orders from their respective governments, Egypt and Surinam refused to play against South Africa. The World Bridge Federation banned both offenders from world bridge events for three years.

In the open series, the field was divided into two pools of 29 teams. The leading four teams from both groups qualified for the semi-finals. They were: Group A, Denmark, Brazil, Taiwan and the Netherlands: Group B, Norway, France, USA and Idonesia. France and the United States qualified for the final.

The final was closely contested, with both teams playing bridge of high quality. France took an early lead, but the United States drew level when a French player removed his partner's double only to suffer a heavy penalty himself. The hand that decided the match presented Robert Hamman of the USA with an unusual and critical decision. Holding two aces, he had to select which ace to lead against a grand slam. He chose wrong and France went on to win by 131 IMPS to 111 IMPS.

The performance of the British team was disappointing. Forrester and Smolski, making their debut, played in fine form for the first 15 rounds, but a bad match against Canada appeared to undermine their confidence. Nevertheless they are obviously a good pair with genuine prospects for the future. Priday and Rodrigue started slowly, gradually gathering momentum as the tournament progressed. In the last seven rounds they certainly played with considerable accuracy and aggression. After a pathetic exhibition against Iceland, Sheehan and I had a good run until the last match against Austria, when we played poorly and out of luck.

To see the team's performance in perspective, one must weigh our creditable score of 66 per cent against the uninspiring final classification of 6th in our group. To succeed in an Olympiad, you have to massacre the weak teams, and at least hold your own against the strong ones. To lose 20–0 to Canada, 17–3 to Taiwan, and 13–7 to Brazil, left us with too much ground to recover.

I have always referred to a hand with the top-heavy 8–4–1–0 distribution as an Albatross, which is, I understand, a large ungainly bird capable of remarkable powers of flight. The Bridge Albatross is a rare bird which you may expect to hold only nine times in 20,000 deals. This one occurred in a match between Great Britain and Chile. North–South were game, and dealer was West.

			West	East
♠ Void		♠ A K 7 2	**Flint**	**Sheehan**
♡ A K 9 2	N	♡ 10 7 3	1 ♣	1 ♢
♢ K	W E	♢ A Q 8 7 6 4	2 ♡[1]	2 ♠[2]
♣ A Q J 10 9 8 6 4	S	♣ Void	4 ♣[3]	4 ♢[4]
			5 ♠[5]	7 NT[6]

1 In our system, which has a natural base, the jump in a new suit would generally show support for partner's suit, but as one heart would not have been forcing, I had no attractive alternative. My idea was to dispel the notion of diamond support on the next round.

2 A waiting bid.

3 An attempt to show a powerful independent suit.

4 Meant as a further waiting bid; construed by me as a cue bid, accepting clubs as trumps, and showing a diamond control.

5 Meant as an inquiry about clubs; interpreted by Sheehan as an invitation to bid seven with the diamond AQ.

6 The Albatross is in full flight.

This auction is a fine example of the way even a practised partnership can get its wires crossed. Deservedly, the over-ambitious contract failed by one trick, and we lost 14 IMPs. Luckily, as we still won by 20 VPs–0 VPs, it made no difference to the result of the match, which is more than can be said for my second Albatross.

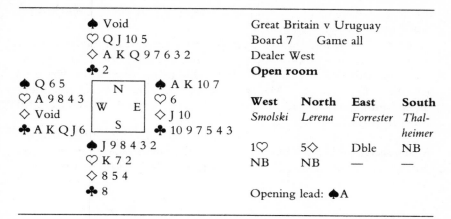

♠ Void
♡ Q J 10 5
◇ A K Q 9 7 6 3 2
♣ 2

♠ Q 6 5
♡ A 9 8 4 3
◇ Void
♣ A K Q J 6

N
W   E
S

♠ A K 10 7
♡ 6
◇ J 10
♣ 10 9 7 5 4 3

♠ J 9 8 4 3 2
♡ K 7 2
◇ 8 5 4
♣ 8

Great Britain v Uruguay
Board 7   Game all
Dealer West
Open room

West	North	East	South
Smolski	Lerena	Forrester	Thal-heimer
1♡	5◇	Dble	NB
NB	NB	—	—

Opening lead: ♠A

On a heart lead, five diamonds can be defeated by two tricks. Not unnaturally, Forrester led the ♠A. After ruffing the opening lead declarer drew trumps and drove out the ♡A. Understandably a little shell-shocked by the turn of events, Smolski failed to cash the ♣A when he obtained the lead with his ♡A, so North made an over-trick. 950 to Uruguay.

The real fireworks were reserved for the closed room.

West	North	East	South
Mayer	Flint	Mrs Mayer	Sheehan
1♡	4◇	5♣	NB
7♣!	Dble	NB	NB
NB	—	—	—

Opening lead: ♡ 2

There were no problems in the play, so that was a further 2,330 points to Uruguay. The total swing was 3,280 or 22 IMPs, the largest swing that I can remember. If Forrester had led a heart in the open room, and Sheehan had led a spade in the closed room, Great Britain would have gained 14 IMPs, which would have changed the result of the match from a loss by 7-13 VPs to a win by 16-4 VPs.

Apart from the choice of leads, I believe there are some instructive points in the bidding. Most text books insist that if you decide to pre-empt, you should do so to the limit. My decision to bid only four diamonds was influenced by the understanding that Sheehan and I have, whereby a double by a player who has made a pre-emptive bid is merely competitive. This arrangement enables the player with the best picture of the hand as a whole to make the final decision. With my strong hearts, I felt this was the best treatment on a hand which might well contain violent distributional storms.

Many critics would endorse Smolski's pass of five diamonds doubled; I do not. A player who pre-empts is inviting a penalty double. If I have a solid side suit which I have not been able to mention, I am chary of accepting these doubles. Mayer knew that the match had been going against him, and his bid of seven clubs was a spirited and successful attempt to turn the tide.

Before Valkenburg, I did not share the mariner's superstition that the Albatross is a bird of ill omen. Now, I would prefer to stare at a new moon through glass, or walk under a dozen ladders, than hold another wretched Albatross.

FIVE

'Give me the cards, I'll play 'em as well as anyone'

Bridge players of all standards are immeasurably conceited. Proof of this is the determination of some rabbits to play the hand at any cost. Although it may not appear in the Guinness Book of Records, one of my partners recently insisted on playing the hand himself in No Trumps rather than support my suit in which he held a hundred honours. When someone (not I) ventured to criticise him, he replied: 'When I come to this club, I know I am going to lose, so I might as least get a little fun for my money.'

To be fair, I suppose everyone enjoys playing the hand. To some, the sense of mastery that the control of both hands gives, is an irresistible lure.

The good dummy player requires a rich assortment of talents. He must possess a sound technique, but also the judgement to recognize when to abandon technique in favour of a psychological or deceptive stroke. He must be adept at concealing whether the contract is iron clad, or requires a miracle. Above all, he must know what is going on at the table.

'Have a good nose', as Garozzo puts it. There are several players who have most of these attributes, but very few who have them all. Benito Garozzo is one.

Speed versus subtlety

There are two types of expert dummy players: 'plunderers' and 'dissectors'. The plunderer uses a blend of speed and psychology to mesmerise his opponents, like a conjurer who takes a watch without his victim noticing. Konstam was a most dangerous exponent of this style. Today any defender who relaxes his attention when Rose, Collings or Hoffman is playing the hand is likely to regret it.

Although the defence is perfectly entitled to play at its preferred tempo, in practice it requires great experience to do so. Usually the plunderer persuades the defenders to play at his pace. Inevitably, they either make mistakes or, equally fatal, they dither, giving declarer valuable information. Possibly the plunderers themselves make the occasional error because they play so fast. But the mistakes that their speed induces in others give them a handsome profit on balance.

The dissectors strive by the exercise of superior technique to take the points which rightfully belong to them. I do not suggest that dissectors are without guile, rather that they place the emphasis on taking the best mathematical chance as opposed to lulling their opponents into error. That is the style of Reese, Forquet and Sheehan.

Although Robert Sheehan's academic life at Oxford was devoted to the study of physiology, I accept his explanation that he is nevertheless a PhD. My dog, however, aware perhaps that Sheehan is a leading dissector, continues to greet him with obvious suspicion. Here is a hand which Sheehan played in the British Bridge League Trials.

```
                    ♠ Q 9 4
                    ♡ A 6 4 3 2
                    ◇ J 9 4 2
                    ♣ A
  ♠ A 10 5 2    ┌─────────┐   ♠ K 8
  ♡ Q 10 9 8 5  │    N    │   ♡ J
  ◇ 3           │  W   E  │   ◇ K 10 8 7 6 5
  ♣ 5 4 3       │    S    │   ♣ Q 8 7 6
                └─────────┘
                    ♠ J 7 6 3
                    ♡ K 7
                    ◇ A Q
                    ♣ K J 10 9 2
```

Teams of four   North-South game

Dealer South

West	North	East	South
	Rose		Sheehan
—	—	—	1♣
NB	1♡	NB	1♠
NB	2◇	Dble	2NT
NB	3NT	NB	NB
NB	—	—	—

Opening lead: ◇ 3

In response to his partner's lead directing double, West led the ♢3. From the diamonds in dummy Sheehan was able to deduce that the suit was distributed 6-1. Obviously he had to develop the clubs, so he crossed to dummy with the ♣A. Now came the first critical decision; with which red suit should he re-enter his hand? Correctly, he decided that there could be no danger from the diamonds, because if the defence tried to establish the suit they would provide him with his ninth trick in the process. As anticipated, West did not follow to the second round of diamonds. He discarded a small club.

Sheehan continued with the ♣K and ♣J, which lost to East's ♣Q, West discarding a heart. East switched to the ♡J, presenting Sheehan with a second vital decision: in which hand should he take the heart? Sheehan took stock of the distribution. He knew that originally East had six diamonds and four clubs, which left room for only three cards in the majors. If East had two hearts and one spade, then provided that he won dummy's ♡A and played a spade, the defenders would be powerless, for regardless of the position of the spade honours they would be unable to enjoy both a heart trick and the ♢K.

Sheehan calculated that if East had started with two spades and one heart he would not even have to guess correctly because East would be on play, forced to concede the ninth trick to dummy's ♢J.

'But suppose West had the ♠AK and ♡Qxxxx?' I objected.

'In that case,' said Sheehan, 'even you would probably have overcalled one heart on the West hand.'

The next hand will appeal to the technicians, for it contains an unusual theme. I will present it as a single dummy problem.

♠ J 9 7 6		Teams	Love all
♡ A J 8		Dealer North	
♢ A 4 3			
♣ J 3 2			

West	North	East	South
—	1NT[1]	NB	4♣[2]
NB	4♠[3]	NB	6♡
NB	NB	NB	—

♠ 10
♡ K Q 10 9 7 6
♢ K Q 5
♣ A K 4

Opening lead: ♠ K

1 An especially weak no trump.
2 Gerber – asking for aces.
3 Two aces.

99

The bidding is not recommended.

When the ♠K held the first trick, West continued with the ♠2 and declarer ruffed East's ♠A. How should declarer proceed? Leaving aside the improbable chance that West had ♠KQ2, there are two possible distributions which will enable declarer to make his contract. Either the ♣Q must drop in two rounds or West must hold five clubs in addition to the ♠Q, in which case he can be squeezed. Notice that it is not enough that West should hold the ♣Q because shortage of entries to dummy would preclude the ♣J from becoming a menace.

To enjoy both chances, the play must be exact. Declarer continues with two rounds of trumps, ending in dummy. He ruffs a spade in his hand and cashes a third round of hearts. Now he plays the ♢KQ and the ♣A. This is the four card ending:

♠ J
♡ —
♢ A
♣ J 3

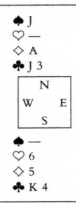

♠ —
♡ 6
♢ 5
♣ K 4

From this novel form of discovery play declarer will learn that one of the two original possibilities can be excluded. For example if West has followed to three rounds of hearts, and to both the ♢K and the ♢Q, because he is known to have at least four spades *it is impossible for him to hold five clubs.* Therefore declarer must play to drop the ♣Q. If West has followed to two rounds of hearts but has discarded on the second round of diamonds, since he can have at most five spades, *he must hold five clubs.*

So declarer cashes his last trump, discarding a club from dummy, and continues with a diamond to dummy's ♢A. West is squeezed and is forced to discard either the ♠Q or from the ♣Q.

The way to look for clues

Mathematicians, contrary to popular belief, are not usually good bridge players. Naturally, if a problem turns on pure technique or on the correct assessment of the odds, the mathematician will usually solve it without difficulty. But it seems that psychology and camouflage are less compatible with calculus.

Doctors, I find, lack the necessary concentration, probably because they are quite properly considering other more serious matters. The world of commerce provides some outstanding players, such as timber merchant Tony Priday and stockbroker Claude Rodrigue, but the occasional moderate player as well. I shall not forget the tycoon of Throgmorton Street who had a penchant for psychic bidding. In answer to an exasperated partner, he explained: 'If I deceive two opponents at the expense of misleading one partner, that must surely show a profit'. It didn't.

In the old days, the Law was the most prolific source of bridge experts. Today, many of the leading younger players seem to come from the world of computers. As bridge is more a game of inference and detection than pure technique, I have always believed that a team which contained Sherlock Holmes, Miss Marple, Hercule Poirot and Lord Peter Wimsey would prove invincible.

This hand from rubber bridge might have proved the undoing of a senior wrangler, but would have been duck soup for a good detective.

♠ K 9 7		Rubber bridge	Game all	
♡ 7 6 2		Dealer South		
◇ 10 8 7 6 3				
♣ Q 2				

♠ Q 10 5 3	♠ 8 2	**West**	**North**	**East**	**South**

West	North	East	South
—	—	—	2NT
NB	3NT	NB	NB
NB	—	—	—

North hand: ♠ K 9 7, ♡ 7 6 2, ◇ 10 8 7 6 3, ♣ Q 2

West hand: ♠ Q 10 5 3, ♡ K J 4, ◇ 9 2, ♣ J 10 9 7

East hand: ♠ 8 2, ♡ 10 9 8 5 3, ◇ J 5 4, ♣ A K 5

South hand: ♠ A J 6 4, ♡ A Q, ◇ A K Q, ♣ 8 6 4 3

Opening lead: ♣ J

Declarer correctly played low from dummy, because if East had ♣Ax he might also play low, which would block the suit. East took the first trick with the ♣K and continued with the ♣A and the ♣5. West cashed his remaining club, on which East discarded the ♡3. After some thought, West switched to the ◇9.

Declarer had a wide choice of plays; the spade finesse, the heart finesse, or the spade-heart squeeze. It is routine technique to begin by cashing the ♠AK to enjoy the chance of dropping the ♠Q, before relying on the heart finesse. Mathematically, the squeeze is against the odds, because to succeed it requires the same hand to hold the ♠Q and the ♡K, and if it is West he must also hold the ♠10 or at least four spades.

How then did declarer select the winning line? Like all good players, he tried to put himself in West's place. The diamond switch is superficially dangerous, possibly destroying any tenace East might have in the suit.

When there is only one entry in dummy, the switch is not just dangerous, but potentially suicidal unless West could be certain that *East could not have any diamond honours.* What could enable him to arrive at that conclusion? Only the knowledge that *he himself held the remainder of the defence's high cards.* Relying on this inference, declarer cashed the ♠AK, then all the diamonds, which squeezed West in the major suits.

The clue on the next hand was far from obvious.

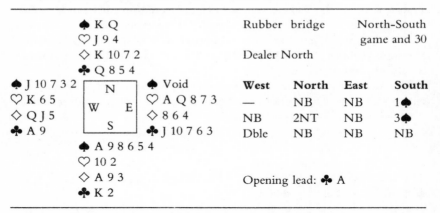

	♠ K Q	Rubber bridge	North-South
	♡ J 9 4		game and 30
	◇ K 10 7 2	Dealer North	
	♣ Q 8 5 4		

	♠ J 10 7 3 2	♠ Void
	♡ K 6 5	♡ A Q 8 7 3
	◇ Q J 5	◇ 8 6 4
	♣ A 9	♣ J 10 7 6 3

	♠ A 9 8 6 5 4
	♡ 10 2
	◇ A 9 3
	♣ K 2

West	North	East	South
—	NB	NB	1♠
NB	2NT	NB	3♠
Dble	NB	NB	NB

Opening lead: ♣ A

East unwisely played the ♣7 on the first trick. This induceed West to continue with the ♣9, which declarer won with the ♣K. Declarer crossed to dummy with the ♠Q, on which East discarded a club, and cashed the ♠K, East throwing the ◇4. When declarer played the ♣Q West mistakenly decided not to ruff, discarding the ♡5. Attempting a trump end play against West, South played a heart, with the idea of extracting West's exit cards. East won with the ♡A and persevered with the ♣J, ruffed by declarer with the ♠8, and overruffed by West with the ♠10. West got off play with the ♡K, which South ruffed with the ♠6. South continued with the ◇A and the ◇9 on which West contributed the ◇Q.

When he won the trick with dummy's ◇K, declarer faced a critical decision in this three card ending.

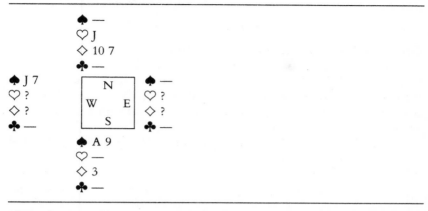

If West's original hand contained three cards in each red suit, the successful line was to continue with a third diamond, putting West on play to lead up to his spade tenace. But if, originally, West had four hearts and only ◇Qx, declarer could make his ninth trick by ruffing a heart, which West would be unable to overruff. Perhaps you think it was a guess? For this declarer it was not. He remembered Hercule Poirot's maxim, 'use the little grey cells'.

Searching for a clue, he recapitulated the play from the beginning. It was true that West's discards were not especially illuminating, *but East's were*. If his original holding in the red suits was ♡AQ87, ◇J864, he would certainly have thrown a heart rather than the ◇4. It followed that West must have started with three cards in each red suit.

Craftmanship

A finesse, according to the dictionary, is a subtlety of contrivance, an artifice, or a crafty trick. Like so many other things today the word has suffered some devaluation. To say of a player 'he will do anything to avoid a finesse' is considered a compliment. Bridge players tend to forget that we inherited the word from whist, where with no dummy exposed the play required more judgement.

Before discussing hands where a finesse may grandly be termed a subtlety of contrivance, let me ask how you should play this everyday suit. You may assume that you have no problems with entries.

A K J 10 7 2   9 8

Of course, it is correct to finesse rather than attempt to drop the Queen. But should you play off one high honour to guard against the singleton Queen, or finesse on the first round? If you think about it, you must select the first round finesse, which gains on four occasions (where North has any small singleton), and loses only once when North has the Queen alone.

On this hand I was North, playing with a conservative bidder but normally sound card player.

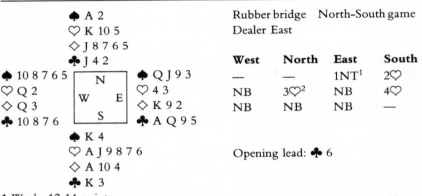

♠ A 2
♡ K 10 5
◇ J 8 7 6 5
♣ J 4 2

♠ 10 8 7 6 5   ♠ Q J 9 3
♡ Q 2   ♡ 4 3
◇ Q 3   ◇ K 9 2
♣ 10 8 7 6   ♣ A Q 9 5

♠ K 4
♡ A J 9 8 7 6
◇ A 10 4
♣ K 3

Rubber bridge   North-South game
Dealer East

West	North	East	South
—	—	1NT[1]	2♡
NB	3♡[2]	NB	4♡
NB	NB	NB	—

Opening lead: ♣ 6

1 Weak, 12-14 points.
2 Aggressive, but justified by the vulnerability.

East took the first trick with the ♣A and returned the ♣5. Declarer tackled trumps immediately, playing to the ♡K and finessing the ♡J to West's Queen. West switched to a spade. Mistakenly presuming that East must have the ◇KQ to account for his opening bid, South won with the ♠K and played a low diamond to the ◇J and ◇K.

When East returned a spade to dummy's ♠A, declarer took a diamond finesse, permitting West to score his doubleton Queen. South, my partner, felt that he could have done better.

'Was I wrong to take the trump finesse?' he asked disconsolately.

'By no means', I replied.

'Then perhaps I shouldn't have played the diamonds like that?'

'No, that is not where you went wrong. As I said, it was correct to take the trump finesse, but only after you had eliminated the black suits. After

104

you won the second trick with the ♣K, you should have continued with two rounds of spades, ending in dummy, then ruffed dummy's last club, and only now play the ♡K and finesse the ♡J.

'The heart finesse may lose, but it has become a *safety play*. West is on play, and he must either concede a ruff and discard or open up the diamonds, which restricts your losses to three tricks in all.'

On my next hand South was a little aggressive in the bidding, but showed sound technique in the play.

♠ A 8 4	Rubber bridge	Game all
♡ Q 7 6	Dealer South	
◇ A 4		
♣ A Q 10 7 2		

♠ K Q	♠ J 9 7 3		
♡ J 10 9 3	♡ 5		
◇ 10 7 2	◇ J 9 8 6 5 3		
♣ J 8 6 4	♣ 9 5		

♠ 10 6 5 2
♡ A K 8 4 2
◇ K Q
♣ K 3

West	North	East	South
—	—	—	1♡
NB	3♣	NB	3♡
NB	4♡	NB	5◇
NB	6♡	NB	NB
NB	—	—	—

Opening lead: ♠ K

South had a difficult decision after four hearts. Five diamonds was surely best if he was going to bid again. With normal distribution six hearts is a good contract, but when two rounds of trumps revealed the bad break the contract was in jeopardy. Declarer appreciated that to succeed he must dispose of two spades *before* West could ruff. This presupposed that West had four clubs. On that assumption South deferred to the probabilities when, after drawing a third round of trumps, he played the ♣K and finessed the ♣10. Now he was able to discard two spades as West followed suit. The fifth club West ruffed, but that was not enough to defeat the slam.

Artifice, contrivance or whatever, it was certainly a crafty trick.

Not by chance

It is easy to spot an expert declarer from the way he tries to ferret out some hidden extra chance. The average player seeing that his contract depends upon a finesse, is as impatient to try his luck as the inveterate gambler. The expert is more circumspect.

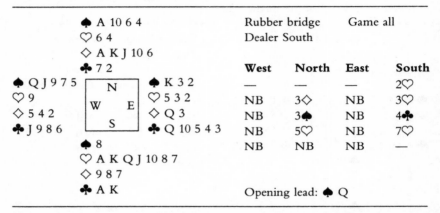

	♠ A 10 6 4		
	♡ 6 4		
	◇ A K J 10 6		
	♣ 7 2		

Rubber bridge — Game all
Dealer South

West	North	East	South
—	—	—	2♡
NB	3◇	NB	3♡
NB	3♠	NB	4♣
NB	5♡	NB	7♡
NB	NB	NB	—

Opening lead: ♠ Q

West: ♠ Q J 9 7 5 ♡ 9 ◇ 5 4 2 ♣ J 9 8 6
East: ♠ K 3 2 ♡ 5 3 2 ◇ Q 3 ♣ Q 10 5 4 3
South: ♠ 8 ♡ A K Q J 10 8 7 ◇ 9 8 7 ♣ A K

Many players would win the ♠A, draw trumps, cash the ◇A and ultimately fall back on the diamond finesse. Unlucky. The correct line is to ruff a spade at trick two, draw trumps, return to dummy with a top diamond and ruff a second spade. Then cash the clubs and run the remaining trumps. This will be the ending:

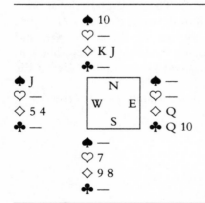

	♠ 10	
	♡ —	
	◇ K J	
	♣ —	

West: ♠ J ♡ — ◇ 5 4 ♣ —
East: ♠ — ♡ — ◇ Q ♣ Q 10
South: ♠ — ♡ 7 ◇ 9 8 ♣ —

On the last trump West discards a diamond while dummy parts with a spade and East with the ♣10. When declarer plays a diamond and West follows with the ◇5, declarer *knows* that the ◇Q must drop because West's last card must be the ♠J.

On the next hand, the exploratory play may be similar but the motive is different.

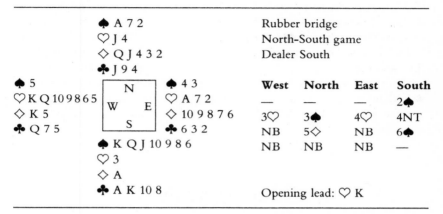

♠ A 7 2
♡ J 4
◇ Q J 4 3 2
♣ J 9 4

♠ 5
♡ K Q 10 9 8 6 5
◇ K 5
♣ Q 7 5

♠ 4 3
♡ A 7 2
◇ 10 9 8 7 6
♣ 6 3 2

♠ K Q J 10 9 8 6
♡ 3
◇ A
♣ A K 10 8

Rubber bridge
North-South game
Dealer South

West	North	East	South
—	—	—	2♠
3♡	3♠	4♡	4NT
NB	5◇	NB	6♠
NB	NB	NB	—

Opening lead: ♡ K

East overtook the ♡K with the ♡A and returned the ♣2. Declarer recognized that although he would probably have to rely on the club finesse, there was a tiny extra chance which it would cost nothing to test. He took the club switch with the ♣A, cashed the ♠K and the ◇A. He crossed to dummy overtaking the ♠J with the ♠A, and ruffed a small diamond with the ♠10. When the ◇K fell, declarer obtained a fine reward for his vision as he crossed to dummy with his carefully preserved ♠6 to discard his two losing clubs on the ◇QJ.

In the final example, some exuberant overbidding had landed declarer in an apparently hopeless contract of six spades.

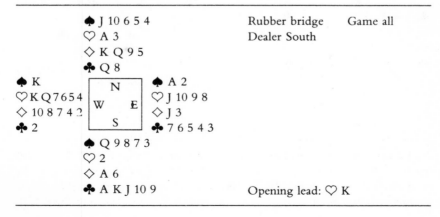

♠ J 10 6 5 4
♡ A 3
◇ K Q 9 5
♣ Q 8

♠ K
♡ K Q 7 6 5 4
◇ 10 8 7 4 2
♣ 2

♠ A 2
♡ J 10 9 8
◇ J 3
♣ 7 6 5 4 3

♠ Q 9 8 7 3
♡ 2
◇ A 6
♣ A K J 10 9

Rubber bridge   Game all
Dealer South

Opening lead: ♡ K

It is obvious that the only chance is to induce a clash of the opposing trump honours. Against a real rabbit, a small spade from hand might catch an unwary West munching the grass. Alternatively, a weak player might rise with the ♠A if declarer starts with the ♠J from dummy. The trouble was that on this occasion both defenders were experienced players. The declarer, Victor Franses, a connoisseur of oriental carpets and a resourceful dummy player, hit upon a clever and original ruse. Whereas he knew that he had only one heart, perhaps the defence did not. Accordingly he played three rounds of diamonds, hoping to give the impression that he was looking for a quick discard. East took the bait, ruffing the ♢Q with the ♠2. Franses overruffed and played a trump with spectacular effect.

I can still hear West's plaintive cry: 'If only you had ruffed with the Ace of spades.'

Taking trouble

Carlyle defines genius as 'the transcendent capacity of taking trouble'. That may be a little sweeping but it provides an admirable guideline for the aspiring bridge player. The hands I shall describe require no genius, only the ability to focus the mind on the critical points and the avoidance of careless error.

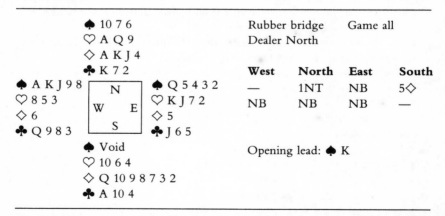

	♠ 10 7 6		
	♡ A Q 9		
	♢ A K J 4		
	♣ K 7 2		

Rubber bridge   Game all
Dealer North

West	North	East	South
—	1NT	NB	5♢
NB	NB	NB	—

♠ A K J 9 8   ♠ Q 5 4 3 2
♡ 8 5 3   ♡ K J 7 2
♢ 6   ♢ 5
♣ Q 9 8 3   ♣ J 6 5

        ♠ Void
        ♡ 10 6 4
        ♢ Q 10 9 8 7 3 2
        ♣ A 10 4

Opening lead: ♠ K

South made a fortunate choice when he jumped to five diamonds over his partner's strong no trump opening. 'Might have missed it, partner', he said gleefully, as he ruffed West's ♠K. He drew the enemy trumps in one round and continued with a heart to dummy's ♡9 which lost to East's ♡J.

East passively returned a spade. As South ruffed he imparted the glad tidings that they had not missed it after all. When the finesse of the ♡Q lost to East's ♡K, South bemoaned the cruel injustice of finding both heart honours badly placed.

'A pity we weren't in six', said North cryptically, 'then the extra 100 would be a small price to pay for the consolation that you had played the hand correctly. As it was you missed a baby elimination play. Ruff the first trick, cross to dummy with a trump, ruff a second spade. Re-enter dummy with a second trump and ruff dummy's last spade. Then play three rounds of clubs. Regardless of the heart distribution, if East wins with the ♡J he will be end played with a choice of conceding a ruff and discard or playing a heart up to dummy's tenace.'

South had another chance on the next hand.

		♠ K 9 6 2			Rubber bridge		Game all	
		♡ 7 4			Dealer East			
		◇ K 10 6 3						
		♣ K J 8						
♠ 4		N		♠ J 10 8 5	**West**	**North**	**East**	**South**
♡ Q J 10 9 8	W		E	♡ 6 5 3 2	—	—	NB	2♣
◇ Q 8 7		S		◇ 4	NB	2NT	NB	3◇
♣ 10 7 6 4				♣ Q 9 5 3	NB	4◇	NB	6◇
		♠ A Q 7 3			NB	NB	NB	—
		♡ A K						
		◇ A J 9 5 2			Opening lead: ♡ Q			
		♣ A 2						

Two rounds of trumps revealed that West had started with ◇Q87. Profiting from his previous unhappy experience, South cashed his remaining high heart and eliminated the clubs before putting West on play with his winning trump. When West switched to a spade, South could not avoid losing a spade.

'After misguessing the diamonds you will agree that I couldn't make that contract', said South complacently.

'Not only could, but should', North replied unkindly. 'If the spades are divided 3-2 the hand is a laydown. Your problem was to provide for the possible 4-1 break. If you had cashed the ♠A before putting West on play, he would have had no spade to lead. If West had had the four spades, he would have been forced to open the suit to your advantage.'

Once more, the cards forgave.

	♠ Q J	Rubber bridge	Game all	
	♡ A J 3	Dealer South		
	◇ K J 10			
	♣ A 10 6 5 3			

	West	**North**	**East**	**South**
	—	—	—	1◇
	NB	2♣	NB	2♠
	NB	4NT	NB	5♡
	NB	6◇	NB	NB
	NB	—	—,	—

West hand: ♠ 5 ♡ K Q 10 9 4 ◇ 5 4 3 ♣ K J 9 8

East hand: ♠ K 10 9 7 6 ♡ 8 7 6 5 2 ◇ 6 ♣ 7 2

South hand: ♠ A 8 4 3 2 ♡ Void ◇ A Q 9 8 7 2 ♣ Q 4

Opening lead: ♡ K

'Thank you, partner, seven's on a finesse', South said as North put down his hand. He won the first trick with dummy's ♡A, discarding a club, and immediately finessed the ♠Q, which won. South opened his mouth to speak.

'Just make six', said North through gritted teeth.

East covered dummy's ♠J with the ♠K and West ruffed South's ♠A.

West switched to a trump. It dawned on South too late that there were now only two trumps in dummy to ruff his three losing spades. In the vain hope that the clubs would divide 3-3, he cashed the ♣A and ruffed a club. He returned to dummy with a trump. The third round of clubs revealed that there was to be no salvation from that suit.

'Don't tell me I could have made that contract', he pleaded pitifully.

'Evidently you could not.'

'Thank goodness', said South, considerably consoled.

'That is to say', North continued, 'an unambitious player who was content to make his contract without an overtrick could have succeeded. Such a player would have withheld his ♠A on the second round of the suit, and subsequently ruffed his two losing spades in dummy. But the fire of your noble optimism is unquenchable'.

110

Unsuitable bunkers at Biarritz

Gary Player's uncanny accuracy from the bunker has saved him countless shots during his illustrious golfing career. In the World Knock-out Teams Championship in Biarritz, Sheehan and I took it in turns, by some wayward bidding, to put each other 'in the sand', and then compounded these inaccuracies by less than perfect play.

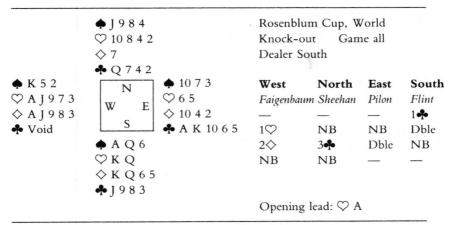

♠ J 9 8 4
♡ 10 8 4 2
♢ 7
♣ Q 7 4 2

♠ K 5 2
♡ A J 9 7 3
♢ A J 9 8 3
♣ Void

♠ 10 7 3
♡ 6 5
♢ 10 4 2
♣ A K 10 6 5

♠ A Q 6
♡ K Q
♢ K Q 6 5
♣ J 9 8 3

Rosenblum Cup, World
Knock-out   Game all
Dealer South

West	North	East	South
Faigenbaum	*Sheehan*	*Pilon*	*Flint*
—	—	—	1♣
1♡	NB	NB	Dble
2♢	3♣	Dble	NB
NB	NB	—	—

Opening lead: ♡ A

Sheehan's bid of three clubs was certainly venturesome, but my re-opening double showed a good hand. West persisted with a second heart, which I won with the ♡K and played the ♢Q. West took his ♢A and switched to the ♠2. Dummy's ♠8 was covered by East's ♠10 and my ♠Q. I ruffed a diamond in dummy and tried the spade finesse. West took the ♠K and played a third round of the suit, a slight error which unhappily I left unpunished. Unwisely, I cashed the ♢K and ruffed my last diamond with dummy's ♣Q. When East overruffed and returned the ♣5 I could take that trick in dummy but *my trumps were now too good* as East could afford to play low on the next round, and I was then forced to lead into his tenace.

If instead of cashing the ♢K I had ruffed a small diamond in dummy, and continued with a spade, East's powerful trumps, whether he ruffs high or low, would have produced only two tricks. Since this hand was played in the critical match that we lost against the French, the eventual winners, the extra undertrick was an expensive mistake.

The second hand occurred in an earlier round.

```
              ♠ K 8                    North-South game
              ♡ 9 4                    Dealer South
              ◇ A 7 6 5
              ♣ A 8 7 6 5          West    North   East    South
  ♠ 5 3 2        ┌───────┐ ♠ 10 9 7 6     Flint           Sheehan
  ♡ J 6        N │       │ ♡ A K Q 10 8 5 3  —      —      —      1◇
  ◇ 10 8 4 2  W ┤       ├ E ◇ Q        NB      2♣      4♡     NB
  ♣ J 9 3 2      │   S   │ ♣ Q         NB      5◇      NB     NB
              └───────┘             NB      —       —      —
              ♠ A Q J 4
              ♡ 7 2
              ◇ K J 9 3
              ♣ K 10 4                Opening lead: ♡ J
```

Despite the temptations of the vulnerability, my five diamonds bid is bad because my hand lacks the intermediates in the minors. East took two top hearts, and switched to a spade which Sheehan won in dummy. A small diamond produced East's ◇Q and Sheehan sensed his fate, which was confirmed when he played a second diamond to dummy's Ace. He went two down. Although the contract must always fail, Sheehan could have restricted the loss to a one-trick set by the farsighted play of cashing a third round of diamonds and *then* the ♣K. After eliminating the spades, he puts West on play with the fourth diamond in the sure knowledge that he must play a club away from his knave. Sure because East's shape is known to be 4-7-1-1.

Cards of ill omen

The nine of diamonds is often called the curse of Scotland. According to folklore this was the fateful card which was the signal for the massacre of Glencoe. But the nine of diamonds is by no means the only card that the superstitious look on with disfavour. The four of clubs is known as 'the devil's bedposts'; the Ace of spades is a card of ill omen, and there are those who profoundly distrust the knave of clubs. A hand last week has persuaded me that he is indeed an untrustworthy rascal.

```
              ♠ K 6 2
              ♡ A K Q 9 6 2
              ◇ 8 7
              ♣ 9 2
♠ A 5       ┌─────────┐   ♠ 10 8 4 3
♡ 7         │    N    │   ♡ 10 5 4 3
◇ J 9 5 4   │ W     E │   ◇ 10 6 3 2
♣ A 7 6 5 4 3│    S    │   ♣ J
            └─────────┘
              ♠ Q J 9 7
              ♡ J 8
              ◇ A K Q
              ♣ K Q 10 8
```

	Rubber bridge	Game all
	Dealer North	

West	North	East	South
—	1♡	NB	1♠
NB	4♡	NB	4NT
NB	5◇	NB	6NT
Dble	NB	NB	NB

Opening lead: ♣A

North's rebid of four hearts was a gross overstatement. In the excitement of the moment, South overlooked that his side's complement of aces was one too few. West led the ♣A. Observing my ♣J, he continued with another club. A grateful South made the remaining twelve tricks.

'If I had played a discouraging club . . .?' I ventured.

'Oh, then I would have switched, of course', said West.

My unhappy experience was by no means unique. Many years ago, a little old lady found herself on lead against six no trumps. She too had two aces. Normally she would have doubled, but the declarer was none other than the redoubtable Harrison Gray, who, she claimed, always redoubled. She led one ace but did not cash the other. Skid Simon, in his own special argot, denied that the old girl was guilty of *two* monstrous 'chucks'.

'If not intending to lead aces, correct not to duggle.'

On my next hand, imagine that you as North have been lucky enough to cut one of the World's most skilful dummy players.

```
              ♠ A Q 9
              ♡ A Q J 4
              ◇ Q J 10
              ♣ K J 4
♠ K J 10 7  ┌─────────┐   ♠ 6 5 4
♡ 9 8 5 3 2 │    N    │   ♡ K 10 7 6
◇ 2         │ W     E │   ◇ K 3
♣ Q 6 5     │    S    │   ♣ 10 8 7 2
            └─────────┘
              ♠ 8 3 2
              ♡ Void
              ◇ A 9 8 7 6 5 4
              ♣ A 9 3
```

	Rubber bridge	Love all
	Dealer North	

West	North	East	South
—	2NT	NB	3◇
NB	3NT	NB	4◇
NB	5◇	NB	6◇
NB	NB	NB	—

Opening lead: ♠J

West lead the ♠J. After considerable reflection, declarer plays dummy's ♠A and discards a spade on dummy's ♡A. He continues with the ♡Q which is covered by East with the ♡K. Having caught a glimpse of the opponents' hands you see that with the ♡J established for a second spade discard, either the finesse of the ♣J or the trump finesse would suffice to ensure 12 tricks. Declarer cashes the ◇A and to your horror, continues with a club to dummy's ♣K. Then he cashes the ♡J, discarding his last spade, and ruffs dummy's last heart before exiting with a trump. Unlucky!

This hand is a good illustration of the expert's inherent, sometimes paranoic, dislike of the finesse. There is much to be said for the initial rejection of the spade finesse, and the play of the ◇A was eminently correct. But to prefer the end play to the club finesse was distinctly against the odds. The end play requires the same hand to hold three specific cards, which is 7-1 against, compared with the even money chance of the club finesse.

Recently someone suggested that an expert with a preview of all four hands would always be able to make an accurate prediction of the probable course of events and the final result.

'Not at all', I replied. He gave a deprecating cough which either meant that he disagreed, or that I must be a pretty poor sort of expert.

Trumping your winners

The 'grand coup' derives its imposing title from the days of whist rather than any inherent technical difficulty. Although there are 13 tricks in no trumps, South has stumbled into seven spades with these cards:

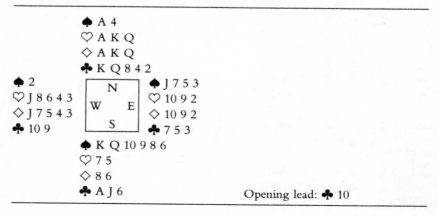

```
              ♠ A 4
              ♡ A K Q
              ◇ A K Q
              ♣ K Q 8 4 2
♠ 2                           ♠ J 7 5 3
♡ J 8 6 4 3      N            ♡ 10 9 2
◇ J 7 5 4 3   W     E         ◇ 10 9 2
♣ 10 9           S            ♣ 7 5 3
              ♠ K Q 10 9 8 6
              ♡ 7 5
              ◇ 8 6
              ♣ A J 6          Opening lead: ♣ 10
```

Provided that the spades divide 3-2, there is no problem. If West has ♠Jxxx there is no hope. It is only when East has the guarded ♠J that the play is interesting. Declarer wins the first trick in his hand with the ♣A. He crosses to dummy's ♠A and returns a spade to his ♠Q. With no more spades in dummy, declarer cannot capture East's ♠J by a straightforward finesse. He can still recover if he can arrange to be in dummy at trick 11. Then when he plays a plain card, East's apparent trump trick is swallowed by declarer's major tenace.

To achieve this ending, declarer must reduce his trumps to the same number as East's. He plays three rounds of hearts, *ruffing the ♡Q*. He follows with three rounds of diamonds, again *ruffing dummy's winning ♢Q*. He returns to dummy with the ♣Q. When East follows to the ♣K declarer is home.

The only difference between a 'grand coup' and a 'trump coup' is that declarer ruffs winners to reduce his trumps.

Hands which involve a trump reduction often afford opportunities for skilful play by both sides.

	♠ K Q 10 9 6			Rubber bridge	East-West game	
	♡ 10 3			Dealer East		
	♢ Q 5					
	♣ K 9 8 6					

♠ A J 5 3		♠ 7 4	**West**	**North**	**East**	**South**
♡ Void	N	♡ K Q 9 4 2	—	—	NB	1♡[1]
♢ A 10	W E	♢ J 4 3 2	Dble[2]	Redble	NB	2♢[3]
♣ A Q J 10 7 5 3	S	♣ 4 2	4♣[4]	Dble	NB	4♢[5]
	♠ 8 2		NB	4♡	Dble	NB
	♡ A J 8 7 6 5		NB	NB	—	—
	♢ K 9 8 7 6					
	♣ Void		Opening lead: ♠ A			

1 A dubious gambit, even at this vulnerability.

2 Too strong for three clubs, a call which has the additional defect of 'losing' the spade suit. The spectre of the final contract becoming one heart doubled is a rare apparition amongst good players.

3 Having opened with sub-minimum values, it is South's duty to warn his partner that he should not expect too much defensive strength.

4 Tempting, but imprudent. If North-South have a fit in a red suit, it has already become apparent. The pre-empt gives the opponents an additional option.

5 This is wrong! I suspect that South trusted West's bidding more than his partner's judgment.

The bidding may have been imperfect but the play was excellent. West led

115

the ♠A and continued with the ♠3. Reasoning that West must have four spades to justify his bidding, South bravely finessed dummy's ♠9. He next played dummy's ♠K and overruffed East's ♡2 with the ♡5.

When South played the ◇6, West faced a critical decision. Appreciating that South needed entries to dummy to reduce his trumps, West took the ◇A and persisted with the ◇10. If he had played low on the first diamond, he would have been put on lead with the ◇A two tricks later, with nothing but black cards to play. When South continued with dummy's ♠Q, it was East's turn to come under pressure. Foreseeing the ending, he discarded a diamond, preserving his ♡KQ94. Although declarer's diamonds were established, he lacked one vital entry to pick up East's trumps.

The next hand was played in the festive spirit of Christmas week. South was an excellent player who has earned the soubriquet of 'the Piranha'. East made no secret that the office party had been a most convivial occasion.

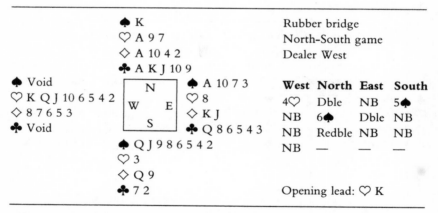

	♠ K	
	♡ A 9 7	Rubber bridge
	◇ A 10 4 2	North-South game
	♣ A K J 10 9	Dealer West

♠ Void
♡ K Q J 10 6 5 4 2
◇ 8 7 6 5 3
♣ Void

♠ A 10 7 3
♡ 8
◇ K J
♣ Q 8 6 5 4 3

♠ Q J 9 8 6 5 4 2
♡ 3
◇ Q 9
♣ 7 2

West	North	East	South
4♡	Dble	NB	5♠
NB	6♠	Dble	NB
NB	Redble	NB	NB
NB	—	—	—

Opening lead: ♡ K

A bystander, attracted by the sounds of hilarity, hurried across the room.
    'What's the contract?' he asked.

'The Piranha is in six spades redoubled', East replied, gloatingly showing his hand to the spectator.

Declarer won the opening lead with dummy's Ace, and paused to reflect. East's demeanour made it clear that he must have all the missing spades. The only hope was a trump reduction to reduce his spades to four. But dummy had one entry too few, and there was also the problem of his losing diamond.

Pure technique would not suffice; declarer needed some cooperation from East. At trick two he ruffed a heart, returned to dummy with a club and ruffed a second heart. On the hearts, East had parted with two clubs.

Declarer continued with a club to dummy's ♣K and played the ♣J, which East covered and declarer ruffed. Then he played a spade, which East won with the ♠A.

This was the six-card ending:

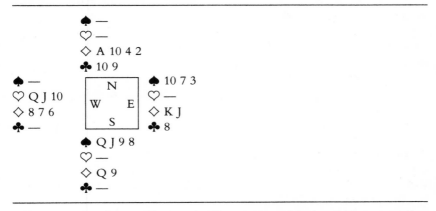

'Doesn't matter how you wriggle, I've got you this time!' East crowed as he blithely got off play with a 'safe' club. Declarer discarded a diamond; then he played dummy's last club. Poor East; the elation of a moment before gave way to a perplexed frown as he discarded the ◇J. South ruffed the club and returned to dummy's ◇A. As declarer held ♠ QJ9, East's second trump trick vanished.

No one mentioned that East could have defeated the contract by playing a diamond instead of a club. Three of the players had not noticed, and the Piranha believed in leaving his opponents happy, if a little poorer.

Tricks and assets

'There's many a man walking the Embankment because he failed to draw trumps', says the old adage; 'and even more who have exchanged riches for rags because they drew trumps too soon', one might reply.

There are two prime reasons for electing to play in a trump contract; one is to maintain control, the other to use the trump suit itself to manufacture extra tricks. Only in the former case is it correct to draw trumps immediately. More commonly, declarer will need to score a ruff in dummy, or rely on a cross ruff.

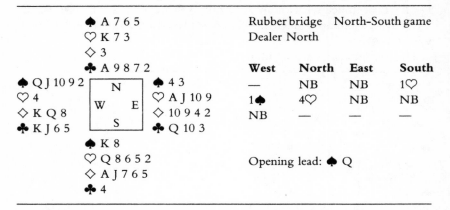

	♠ A 7 6 5		
	♡ K 7 3		
	◇ 3		
	♣ A 9 8 7 2		

Rubber bridge   North-South game
Dealer North

West	North	East	South
—	NB	NB	1♡
1♠	4♡	NB	NB
NB	—	—	—

Opening lead: ♠ Q

North-South were playing five-card majors, which explains North's immediate jump to four hearts. One of the advantages of the method is that you can go straight to the final contract without painting unnecessarily revealing pictures on the way.

Some players misplay this type of hand because they refuse to take proper stock of their assets. The choice lies between establishing one of the minor suits or playing on cross ruff lines. South wisely selected the cross ruff. He won the lead in his hand with the ♠K, cashed the ◇A and ruffed a diamond in dummy. He cashed dummy's ♠A and ♣A and continued with a club, which he ruffed in hand. A second diamond ruff and a second club ruff left this end position, South having made eight tricks.

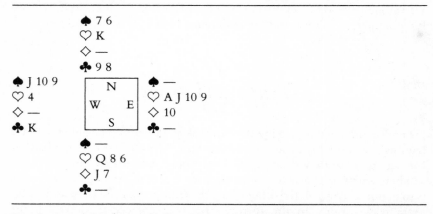

South played the ◇J, ruffed by West, and over-ruffed with dummy's ♡K. Despite his powerful trumps, East could not prevent South from making ten tricks.

118

The next hand is an echo of the same theme.

```
          ♠ A K 8 4              Rubber bridge      Game all
          ♡ A 9 7 6 4           Dealer South
          ◇ 5
          ♣ K 9 3               West    North   East    South
♠ J 10 7       ┌─────┐  ♠ 9 6 5 3   —       —       —       1◇
♡ Q 10 8       │  N  │  ♡ K J 3 2
◇ K 10 9 4 3 W │     │ E ◇ Q 8      NB      1♡      NB      2♣
♣ 6 2          │  S  │  ♣ Q 7 4     NB      2♠¹     NB      3♣
               └─────┘              NB      4♣²     NB      5♣
          ♠ Q 2                     NB      6♣      NB      NB
          ♡ 5                       NB      —       —       —
          ◇ A J 7 6 2
          ♣ A J 10 8 5
                                    Opening lead: ♠ J
```

1 The fourth suit, forcing, asking South to describe his hand.
2 The raise is forcing, because if it were not, South after the fourth suit would always be expected to make futile little jumps to indicate any extra values, the epitome of bad bidding.

Declarer faces a difficult choice. Should he seek to develop the diamonds, reverse the dummy by establishing the hearts, or rely on a cross ruff? The plan of reversing the dummy is completely unworkable, because it requires three heart ruffs and one spade ruff in hand and no less than four entries in dummy. Furthermore, if dummy is to be the master hand, one must not weaken the trump length by taking diamond ruffs in dummy.

Developing the diamonds is a superficially more promising notion, but deeper analysis reveals that declarer would lose trump control. The only genuine hope for this ambitious contract is a cross ruff. Provided declarer can cash five side suit winners (♠AKQ, ◇A, ♡A) he will require seven tricks from the trump suit.

It is a good exercise in technique. Declarer wins the first trick with the ♠Q, crosses to dummy with the ♡A, and ruffs a heart with the ♣5. He returns to dummy with the ♠K and cashes the ♠A. Now comes a diamond to the ◇A, and a diamond ruffed with dummy's ♣3. Declarer has made seven tricks. He is home provided he does not sustain an unnecessary over-ruff.

He ruffs a heart with the ♣8, and then ruffs a diamond *with the ♣K*. He ruffs a heart *with the ♣A*. The combination of declarer's ♣J10 and dummy's ♣9 are sufficient to guarantee the two tricks that he requires. South's play had to be precise to justify his partner's optimistic bidding.

Making dummy the master hand

The play of a suit contract will often depend upon the correct manipulation of the trumps. Players sometimes have a blind spot, especially where the winning line consists in establishing the dummy. The following hand surprisingly deceived an international player.

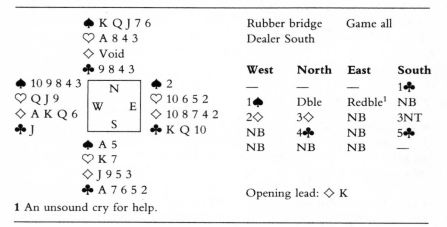

	♠ K Q J 7 6			Rubber bridge	Game all		
	♡ A 8 4 3			Dealer South			
	◇ Void						
	♣ 9 8 4 3						

West	North	East	South
—	—	—	1♣
1♠	Dble	Redble[1]	NB
2◇	3◇	NB	3NT
NB	4♣	NB	5♣
NB	NB	NB	—

West hand: ♠ 10 9 8 4 3 ♡ Q J 9 ◇ A K Q 6 ♣ J

East hand: ♠ 2 ♡ 10 6 5 2 ◇ 10 8 7 4 2 ♣ K Q 10

South hand: ♠ A 5 ♡ K 7 ◇ J 9 5 3 ♣ A 7 6 5 2

Opening lead: ◇ K

1 An unsound cry for help.

Declarer ruffed the lead in dummy and with the mistaken notion of keeping trump control, ducked a club to West. West switched to the ♡Q, which declarer won in hand with the ♡K. Declarer crossed to dummy with a diamond ruff, cashed the ♡A and ruffed a heart. A further diamond ruff was followed by the ♣A.

Unhappily when the trumps failed to divide, East was able to ruff the second spade and play a diamond for the setting trick. Do you see where declarer went wrong?

The hand belongs to a common genus where the correct technique is to leave one or two enemy trumps at large while you cross ruff or establish the dummy. Provided the trumps are no worse that 3-1 you can cash the ♣A at trick two and *put your hand down claiming 11 tricks.* If your opponents ask you to amplify your line of play, you explain that two rounds of hearts and a heart ruff are followed by the Ace of spades and a spade to the King. If East ruffs and draws a second round of trumps, dummy will contain a trump, two winning spades, a spade loser, and a heart loser, but your hand has two trumps to take care of those losers. The irreparable error was the second diamond ruff, *which prematurely removed a vital entry to dummy.*

Here is another deceptive specimen for those unaccustomed to making dummy the master hand.

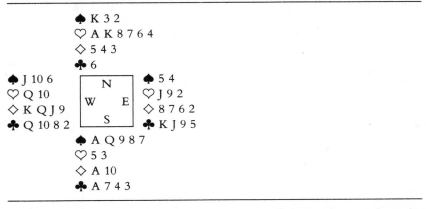

South, playing in the adventurous contract of six spades, receives the inconvenient lead of the ◇K. On a club lead he could duck a heart, but that line is obviously no longer available. The weak player would cash the ♣A and ruff a club before looking round the field, and his normal expectancy would be precisely eleven tricks. But to make the slam requires only normal breaks in the major suits. This is the winning line. Win with the ◇A, cash the ♡AK and ruff a heart with the ♠Q. Cash the Ace and King of spades, then play hearts. West ruffs, but declarer discards his diamond. Dummy's ♠3 provides the vital entry to enjoy the remaining hearts. Five hearts, effectively five spades, and two minor aces add up to a rewarding twelve tricks.

Whenever a straightforward plan does not reveal a way to make the contract, always examine the possibility of reversing the dummy. It is an invaluable habit.

When success smells sweetest

Complacency and despair may be complementary, but at the bridge table they represent opposing poles in a common theme. You should be constantly on your guard against both these dangerous attitudes. If a contract appears to be simple and straightforward, the good player will try to envisage any hidden snags, and then strive to circumvent them. In this hand declarer encountered a most unusual position without any prior warning.

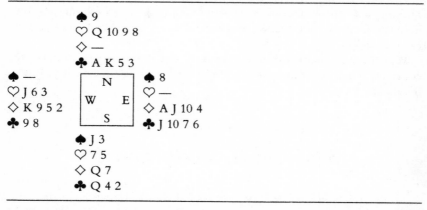

North hand:
♠ 9 7 6 4
♡ Q 10 9 8 4
◇ Void
♣ A K 5 3

West hand:
♠ 10 2
♡ A J 6 3
◇ K 9 5 3 2
♣ 9 8

East hand:
♠ Q 8 5
♡ 2
◇ A J 10 8 4
♣ J 10 7 6

South hand:
♠ A K J 3
♡ K 7 5
◇ Q 7 6
♣ Q 4 2

Rubber bridge   North–South game
Dealer South

West	North	East	South
—	—	—	1♣
NB	1♡	NB	1♠
NB	3◇	Dble	3♠
NB	4♠	NB	NB
NB	—	—	—

Opening lead: ♠ 2

North's jump in the fourth suit (three diamonds) confirmed South's second suit as trumps. This interpretation explains South's rebid of three spades, which was merely marking time, and not a descriptive bid. East played the ♠Q on the first trick, and declarer won with the ♠K. He drew a second round of trumps with the ♠A, and then played the ♡K which West took with the ♡A. West switched to the ◇3, forcing dummy to ruff. After four tricks this was the position, with the lead in dummy:

North hand:
♠ 9
♡ Q 10 9 8
◇ —
♣ A K 5 3

West hand:
♠ —
♡ J 6 3
◇ K 9 5 2
♣ 9 8

East hand:
♠ 8
♡ —
◇ A J 10 4
♣ J 10 7 6

South hand:
♠ J 3
♡ 7 5
◇ Q 7
♣ Q 4 2

Declarer has lost only one trick. As the cards lie, a successful line is to return to hand with the ♣Q, and take the heart finesse. Although East ruffs, this is the last trick for the defence, as the declarer can ruff one diamond and establish the hearts in order to discard the other. But suppose that East had ♡J2. Now declarer will be forced to ruff a second diamond in dummy. If he fails to guess which suit to cash, the defence will ruff and defeat the contract with a winning diamond. Equally the slap-happy play of the ♡Q would be punished immediately. East would ruff and play a diamond. Declarer could no longer establish the hearts without losing four tricks. His remaining vain hope would be that the clubs were divided.

Oddly, there is a continuation that caters for any distribution, the ♡10. Regardless of which defender wins the trick, declarer's entries are preserved. If a contract appears impossible, do not despair. Try to construct some favourable distribution which will allow you to succeed. It does not matter that the distribution you require is improbable, the occasional success is all the sweeter because of its very rarity.

This remarkable freak which occurred in a practice match before the 1976 Olympiad is a good example. The declarer was Willie Coyle, arguably Scotland's leading player.

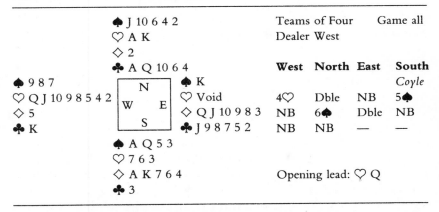

	♠ J 10 6 4 2		Teams of Four		Game all
	♡ A K		Dealer West		
	◇ 2				
	♣ A Q 10 6 4		**West**	**North**	**East**	**South**
♠ 9 8 7		♠ K				*Coyle*
♡ Q J 10 9 8 5 4 2		♡ Void	4♡	Dble	NB	5♠
◇ 5		◇ Q J 10 9 8 3	NB	6♠	Dble	NB
♣ K		♣ J 9 8 7 5 2	NB	NB	—	—
	♠ A Q 5 3				
	♡ 7 6 3				
	◇ A K 7 6 4		Opening lead: ♡ Q
	♣ 3				

Most players accept that a double of four hearts promises support for spades, which explains South's bid of five spades. East doubled to ensure a heart lead.

East ruffed dummy's ♡K with the ♠K and switched to the ◇Q. After winning the diamond with his ◇A, Coyle took stock of his assets. He was convinced that West's distribution must be 3-8-1-1. (If he had two diamonds and a void club he would doubtless have led a small heart as a suit preference signal for a club return.) A cross ruff must fail because of the size of West's spade intermediates. Ruffing two diamonds in dummy would superficially produce only ten tricks.

Suddenly, Coyle saw a chink of light. Suppose West's club was the King. Now he would have eleven tricks and a squeeze in the minor suits would produce the twelfth. Coyle ruffed a diamond in dummy, cashed the ♡A and returned to his hand with the ♠Q. He ruffed a second diamond in dummy, cashed the ♠J, and re-entered his hand with the ♠A. When he played his last trump, East could not resist the pressure.

Notice that Coyle had to rely on his assumption that West had the singleton ♣K. To test this assumption prematurely would have removed a vital entry. This point was not lost on West, who rather harshly criticized his partner for failing to find the entry destroying switch. Coyle had the last word. 'I still make the contract', he assured a disconsolate East. 'After winning the club in dummy I cash the ♡A and enter my hand with the ♠Q. I continue with the ◇A and the ◇4 which I ruff in dummy. Next I play the ♠J. This leaves a six-card ending with the lead in dummy.'

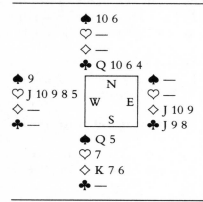

```
              ♠ 10 6
              ♡ —
              ◇ —
              ♣ Q 10 6 4
♠ 9                           ♠ —
♡ J 10 9 8 5      N           ♡ —
◇ —           W     E         ◇ J 10 9
♣ —              S            ♣ J 9 8
              ♠ Q 5
              ♡ 7
              ◇ K 7 6
              ♣ —
```

'When I play the ♠10, what does East discard? If he parts with a club, I can leave the lead in dummy and establish the clubs with one ruff. If he elects to throw a diamond, *I overtake the ♠10 with the ♠Q*, and establish the diamonds. I wish you had returned a club', he concluded, 'you spoilt a pretty hand.'

Priorities first

'First things first,' we were told when we were young. A singularly obstinate child, it was not until much later that I realized the advice was sensible and practical. At the bridge table, the failure to observe a proper sense of priority is the frequent cause of unnecessary defeat. Here is a simple example.

```
            ♠ 10 7 4              Rubber bridge      Game all
            ♡ Q J 10 9           Dealer South
            ◇ K Q J
            ♣ A K 3
♠ K                   ♠ J 9 3     West    North    East    South
♡ 7 6 4      N        ♡ K 8 5 2   —       —        —       1♠
◇ 10 8 7 6  W   E     ◇ 9 5 3     NB      3♣       NB      3♠
♣ Q J 10 9 5    S     ♣ 7 6 2     NB      4♠       NB      6♠
            ♠ A Q 8 6 5 2         NB      NB       NB      —
            ♡ A 3
            ◇ A 4 2               Opening lead: ♣ Q
            ♣ 8 4
```

The final contract is against the odds. Although the old school advocated the use of a forcing take-out on any hand with 16 points or more, there is much to be said for the modern philosophy of reserving the forcing take-out for hands with powerful support or an independent suit.

Declarer won the club lead in dummy and immediately finessed the ♠Q. East's ♠J93 ensured the setting trick for the defence. Declarer was guilty of muddled thinking. To make the contract, he must restrict his losses to either no hearts and one spade or one heart and no spades.

To determine the correct play of the trump suit, declarer's *first* move should be to discover whether he has to lose a heart. When the heart finesse succeeds, declarer can concentrate on minimizing his chances of losing more than one spade. If this suit combination is taken in isolation, the ♠A is a standard safety play. Obviously if the heart finesse loses, the finesse of the ♠Q is the only way to play the suit to lose no tricks.

125

The declarer on the next hand had an exact knowledge of the odds, but little idea how to apply them.

	♠ A Q 10 9		Rubber bridge	Game all
	♡ 8 4		Dealer South	
	◇ K 8 4			
	♣ K 9 6 4			

West	North	East	South
—	—	—	1◇
NB	1♠	NB	2♣
NB	2♡[1]	NB	3NT
NB	NB	NB	—

♠ 8 5
♡ K Q J 9 7
◇ Q 9
♣ J 10 8 7

♠ K 7 6 4 2
♡ 10 6 5 2
◇ 10 7 5
♣ 5

♠ J 3
♡ A 3
◇ A J 6 3 2
♣ A Q 3 2

Opening lead: ♡ K

1 'The fourth suit'. North's bid does not show any strength or length in hearts; it asks South to describe his hand, and bid no trumps if he has the hearts guarded.

Superficially, five clubs appears to be a superior contract. Deeper analysis reveals that three no trumps is better. Declarer learnedly ducked the ♡K in case the hearts were divided seven-two, but was forced to win the heart continuation. He cashed the ♣AQ and learnt the bad news. Now he could only see seven tricks. After an impressively accurate aside that the probability of losing no diamonds was only 34 per cent, declarer took the spade finesse. He was evidently needled by his partner's undisguised lack of approval.

Whereas it is true that the spade suit offers the best chances of making the extra tricks, declarer's argument contained a glaring defect. Before committing himself to the spade finesse he should have cashed the ◇A and ◇K. The combined chances of this line of play add up to 65 per cent, a distinct improvement on the even-money chance of the spade finesse.

My final hand deceived a player who is certainly no novice.

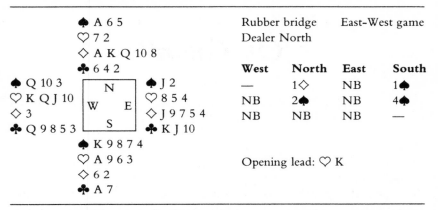

	♠ A 6 5				
	♡ 7 2	Rubber bridge		East-West game	
	◇ A K Q 10 8	Dealer North			
	♣ 6 4 2				

	West	**North**	**East**	**South**
	—	1◇	NB	1♠
	NB	2♠	NB	4♠
	NB	NB	NB	—

West: ♠ Q 10 3 ♡ K Q J 10 ◇ 3 ♣ Q 9 8 5 3

East: ♠ J 2 ♡ 8 5 4 ◇ J 9 7 5 4 ♣ K J 10

South: ♠ K 9 8 7 4 ♡ A 9 6 3 ◇ 6 2 ♣ A 7

Opening lead: ♡ K

South correctly ducked the opening lead and won the heart continuation. He ruffed a heart with dummy's ♠5 and cashed the ♠A and ♠K. If the diamonds had been divided no worse that 4–2, declarer would have been able to discard one of his losers. Unhappily, West ruffed the second round of diamonds and South could not avoid losing a heart and a club, to go one down.

Did you spot South's mistake? It was an error players frequently make. Suppose that instead of taking the heart ruff immediately, South starts with two rounds of trumps. He then turns to the diamonds. As before West ruffs the second round, but the critical difference is that dummy's trump provides the vital entry to the ◇Q.

SIX

'On Guard'

S J Simon once wrote: 'There are any number of excellent dummy players, but only a handful of good defenders.' Very true. Defence is undoubtedly the most difficult element of the game. Unlike the declarer, the defence cannot initially count or see its combined assets. To compensate for this disadvantage, the defenders must signal to each other. But declarer is watching too, so the value of any signal must be measured against the information that it gives away.

To defend well you must sometimes preserve the classic stance with upright guard, and on other occasions catch your opponent with a knock-out counter punch. The judgement of which line to pursue requires skill, inspiration, and a bit of luck.

Getting the signals across

A correspondent takes me to task for neglecting 'the art of useful communication between defenders'. I shall try to repair the omission.

Defence is indeed an art. The harmonic combination of two minds to provide a successful counterpoint gives more intellectual satisfaction than even the most brilliant dummy play. Sadly, players often fall far short of this halcyon ideal because defence is, above all, a *difficult* art.

The declarer starts with a big advantage. Only he can see the total forces at his disposal. The defence can rely initially only on inference, deduction and, later, on signals and discards. Once upon a time a high card was an unambiguous invitation to continue a suit. The moderns have introduced two notions to muddy the waters, distributional and suit preference signals.

Here is a spectacular accident which I hope will persuade you that, where there is any risk of confusion, suit preference signals should not apply to the first trick.

	♠ A 4	Rubber bridge	Game all	
	♡ 4	Dealer South		
	◇ A Q 9 5			
	♣ Q 10 6 5 4 2			

	♠ A 4				
♠ Void		♠ J 6 5 3	**West**	**North**	**East**	**South**

♠ A 4	♡ 4	◇ A Q 9 5	♣ Q 10 6 5 4 2

♠ Void
♡ A J 9 8 6 5
◇ 10 8 7 2
♣ J 9 8

N W E S

♠ J 6 5 3
♡ K 10 7 3
◇ J 6 4 3
♣ 7

♠ K Q 10 9 8 7 2
♡ Q 2
◇ K
♣ A K 3

West	North	East	South
—	—	—	1♠
NB	2♣	NB	4♠[1]
NB	6♠	NB	NB
NB	—	—	—

Opening lead: ♡A

1 As 3♠ would be forcing, 4♠ promised a fit in clubs.

West led the ♡A. Naturally keen to shorten dummy's trumps, East played the ♡10 to encourage West to play a second heart. But West was no simple soul. After due reflection, he switched to a diamond, construing Easts' ♡10 as a suit preference signal.

'How could I have persuaded you to play a second heart?' East squawked.

'Perhaps if you played the ♡K.'

'Rubbish', East cut in, 'You would still have switched to a diamond —
only more quickly.'

Distributional signals have a proper place in the defence's armoury. For
example, it is obviously sensible to signal length in dummy's long suit to
help partner to judge when to take his ace. But distributional signals must
play second fiddle to signals which express encouragement or dis-
couragement, particularly at trick one. Superficially, the correct defence
on the hand which follows may appear to contradict what I have written.

```
            ♠ Q 10 8 7          Teams of four      East-West game
            ♡ Q 6 4             Dealer East
            ◇ A K J
            ♣ Q 9 8
♠ 3                    ♠ 6 5     West    North   East    South
♡ A K 9 8 2   ┌─────┐  ♡ J 10 5 2  —      —      NB      1♠
◇ 7 5 3       │ N   │  ◇ Q 6 4 2  NB     2♣¹     NB      2◇
♣ J 10 7 6   W│     │E ♣ 4 3 2    NB     4♠      NB      5♣
              │  S  │             NB     5◇      NB      6♠
              └─────┘             NB     NB      NB      —
            ♠ A K J 9 4 2
            ♡ 7                   Opening lead: ♡K
            ◇ 10 9 8
            ♣ A K 5
```

1 North, deciding that his hand was too good for a direct bid of four spades,
initiated a 'delayed game raise'. The dangers of using this treatment with only a
three-card suit soon became apparent. South reasonably supposed that his ♣AK
were jewels beyond price, only to find that they were paste.

West led the ♡K, on which East contributed the ♡J. Was it possible, West
wondered, that South had bid six spades with ♡10xx? Most improbable,
he decided; a far more likely construction was that East's signal meant that
he had four hearts. When West switched to the ◇7, South could not avoid
defeat.

Notice that East's ♡J could not be an encouraging signal, because West
held both the top honours himself, and on the bidding South must have
second round heart control.

A useful understanding common to all good players is that the discard of
an honour should always be the top of a sequence. On this hand opposite,
it paved the way to a successful defence.

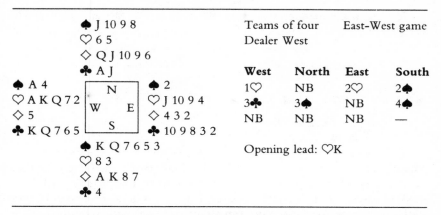

	West	North	East	South
	1♡	NB	2♡	2♠
	3♣	3♠	NB	4♠
	NB	NB	NB	—

Teams of four   East–West game
Dealer West

Opening lead: ♡K

On the lead of the ♡K, East played the ♡J. West switched to his singleton diamond which declarer won in hand with the ◇A. Declarer then made the naive try of a small spade but West alertly took the ♠A and played a small heart enabling East to give him his diamond ruff. Without the assurance that East had the ♡10, West might well have pinned his hopes on making a club trick.

'Well defended', said South sportingly.

'It was played by the wrong hand', said North.

'It wouldn't have made any difference', said South, rising to the bait.

'If *I* had played the hand', North explained immodestly, 'I wouldn't have guilelessly played a spade at trick three. Instead I would have crossed to dummy's ♣A and returned the ♣J, discarding my losing heart.'

Falsely poker-face

The chameleon's ability to change colour is an effective form of protection. The astute defender must learn not only to camouflage his holdings, but also to do so without a give-away hesitation.

The smooth play of the obligatory false card is the expert's stock-in-trade. Less gifted players either fail to play the correct card at all, or play it after a fatal pause.

131

Here is an elementary example. West leads the ♠3 against a spade contract.

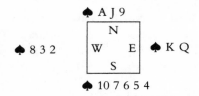

Many players would win with the King because that is their habit. Others would remember the valid general instruction that such false cards will mislead partner more than the declarer. But on this occasion you must win with the *Queen*, because any competent declarer will undoubtedly be capable of drawing the inference that West would not lead from ♠Qxx.

Frequently the defence, by playing the right card, can make declarer guess. Here are a few standard examples of that theme:

South plays the ♠2 finessing dummy's Jack. If East follows with the ♠6 declarer has no choice. He must cash the Ace. But if East contributes the ♠9 on the first round, declarer might well return to hand with the intention of playing the ♠Q to crush East's hypothetical ♠10 9 doubleton.

When a suit is distributed 4-4-4-1, there are many opportunities for the alert defender.

If South plays a small spade to dummy's King, the defence will have no chance of a trick if East follows with the ♠3. But suppose East contributes the ♠9. Now declarer has been provided with the option of guarding against an original holding of ♠J 7 4 3 in the West hand. It is worth noting that declarer should start this particular suit with the ♠K from dummy, rather than a small card up to the King, because the discard of the ♠9 would be costly for the defence should West hold the singleton ♠10.

Here is another suit combination where the defence often misses its chance:

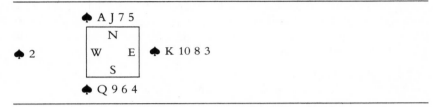

If, when declarer plays a small card to dummy's ♠J, East takes the ♠K, that will be the defence's only trick. But if East contributes the ♠8, declarer might well return to hand to try the effect of playing the Queen.

The J9 can often be used to extract an extra trick.

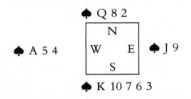

Declarer starts the suit by playing the ♠2 from dummy, covering East's ♠9 with his ♠10. The defence will have to be content with one trick. But suppose on the first round East rises with the ♠J. South plays the ♠K; even a perspicacious declarer may take a losing finesse of the ♠8 on the second round.

This standard example of the so-called obligatory false card is well known.

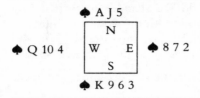

South successfully finesses the Jack. If when declarer continues with dummy's Ace, West contributes the ♠10, declarer has no choice but to drop the Queen. The principle of playing the card you are known to hold is a valuable one, with many applications.

When declarer has a long suit facing a singleton in dummy, it is usually only the most experienced defender who will lead him astray.

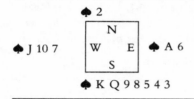

Obviously East should duck, but declarer will have no losing choice unless West contributes the ♠J or ♠10.

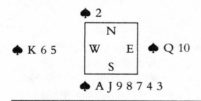

Unless East rises with the Queen, declarer will be forced to make six tricks by covering East's ♠10 with the ♠J.

The false cards I have described can only profit the defence, and should never deceive partner. Such deceptions in no way subtract from my constant plea: 'Heaven protect me from partners who sprinkle false cards like confetti.'

Discard dilemmas

Discard problems are of varying complexity. My first hand is so straightforward that you might be surprised that anyone could go wrong.

```
              ♠ 6 5 4                Rubber bridge     Game all
              ♡ 7 2                  Dealer South
              ◇ J 7 3
              ♣ Q 9 8 6 5
  ♠ 7 2          N       ♠ A 3       West    North    East    South
  ♡ Q 10 8 6             ♡ 5 4 3     —       —        —       2♠
  ◇ A K 9 4   W     E    ◇ 10 8 6 5 2  NB    2NT      NB      3♡
  ♣ K 4 3         S      ♣ J 10 7    NB      3♣       NB      4♠
              ♠ K Q J 10 9 8         NB      NB       NB      —
              ♡ A K J 9
              ◇ Q
              ♣ A 2                  Opening lead: ◇ K
```

West was a solid player; East an expert; and South a good aggressive player, as we shall see, capable of some wily manoeuvres. When East contributed the ◇2 to the opening lead and South dropped the ◇Q, West correctly switched to the ♠2. East took his ♠A and continued with the ♠3. Declarer can make his contract by playing the ♣A and another club, establishing dummy's ♣Q, ruffing a heart in dummy and discarding his last heart on the ♣Q.

However, he embarked on what he believed to be a more elegant line. He cashed the ♡AK and continued with the ♡9, permitting West to hold the trick with the ♡10. This play succeeds if either defender holds ♡Qxx, or if West holds ♡10xx together with the ♣K and the ◇A, which he has already shown by his opening lead.

West would be end played. Either he would have to establish dummy's ◇J or lead away from his ♣K. As it was, West was able to continue with the ♡Q, forcing a ruff in dummy with the ♠6. South's genuine chance had vanished, which exposes the fallacy in his original plan.

Now he had to rely on a defensive error. He returned to hand with the ♣A and rattled off his trumps. On the last trump, West had to part with either the ♣K or the ◇A. After some belated thought he 'guessed' wrong.

There are two instructive points. West was guilty of relaxing his concentration after he had played the ♡Q. It was then that he should have foreseen the critical discard to come. Whereas it was superficially possible that declarer's original hand was:

♠ K Q J 10 x x
♡ A K J 9
♢ Q x
♣ A

logically, it was inconceivable. With this hand, after winning the second spade, declarer would continue with a diamond, establishing dummy's ♢J for a discard of his fourth heart.

Even if West overlooks this simple inference, he should still make the correct decision. You will remember that East was an expert. Although West might not anticipate the sequence of play, East would. It is standard expert technique in these pseudo–squeeze endings to discard one suit completely.

Here it was not physically possible for East to discard all his diamonds. He did the next best thing, following to the first round of clubs with the ♣7 and discarding the ♣10 and the ♣J at the earliest opportunity. This hand reaffirms the truth of the saying: 'Occasionally a good defender may be forced to guess in the early play — but in the end game, never.'

On the next hand, it was essential for West to anticipate declarer's line of play.

	♠ 10 4 2		Pairs	Game all		
	♡ 7 2		Dealer South			
	♢ 8 4					
	♣ A K Q J 10 9					

♠ K Q J 9 8 7		♠ 6 5	**West**	**North**	**East**	**South**
♡ K 6 5	N	♡ J 10 8 3	—	—	—	1♡
♢ 9 3	W E	♢ J 10 7 6 5	1♠	2♣	NB	3NT
♣ 8 3	S	♣ 6 5	NB	6NT	NB	NB
	♠ A 3		NB	—	—	—
	♡ A Q 9 4					
	♢ A K Q 2		Opening lead: ♠ K			
	♣ 7 4 2					

The bidding is typical of the artificial emphasis on no trumps, peculiar to match point pairs. Although six clubs is a far superior contract, the bidding was the same at nearly every other table.

Declarer, a highly competent performer, won the first trick with the ♠A, cashed the three top diamonds and started on the clubs.

Suppose you are West. How would you estimate your chances of defeating the contract? If you are complacently counting on your ♡K and a spade, you are in for a rude shock. Declarer's plan is obvious, or it should be. He intends to run the clubs, reducing the hand to a three card ending.

You will have the choice of denuding your precious ♡K, or coming down to the ♠Q and ♡K6.

If you elect to do the latter, declarer will put you on play with your spade honour to lead up to his heart tenace. But if you envisage the ending, you may outwit him. You are faced with five discards. I suggest that they should be ♣8, ♣9, ♡5, ♡6 and ♠J in that order, leaving yourself with the ♠Q7 and the ♡K. If declarer still attempts the end play, I am sure you will enjoy his look of chagrin as you produce your carefully preserved ♠7.

Take thirteen cards . . .

Mrs Beaton's recipe for good defence would undoubtedly have been 'nine parts application to one part inspiration'. The errors made on the hands I shall discuss may seem mundane and might have passed unnoticed had they not been perpetrated by players of international repute.

	♠ A Q 7		
	♡ J 9 3 2		
	◇ 10 5		
	♣ Q 9 7 5		

♠ J 9 6 2		♠ K 10 3
♡ 8 7	N	♡ Q 4
◇ J 8 7 2	W E	◇ A Q 6 4
♣ 4 3 2	S	♣ A K 10 6

	♠ 8 5 4
	♡ A K 10 6 5
	◇ K 9 3
	♣ J 8

Rubber bridge   East-West game
Dealer East

West	North	East	South
—	—	1◇	1♡
NB	3♡	Dble	4♡
NB	NB	Dble	NB
NB	NB	—	—

Opening lead: ◇ 2

North's bid of three hearts was decidely aggressive, South's four hearts even more so, and East's final double ill-advised. East won the ◇A, and seeing no danger to his four 'certain' tricks returned the ◇4.

Declarer won with the ◇K and cashed the two top trumps. He continued with his last diamond, which he ruffed in dummy. When declarer played a low club from dummy, East belatedly saw the danger. The ♣Q would provide declarer with his ninth trick, and after taking the ♣A and ♣K, East would be unable to avoid giving him his tenth. Either

137

he would have to lead up to one of dummy's black tenaces or play a diamond, conceding a ruff and discard.

'Perhaps I should have led a spade', said West deferentially.

To his credit, East was quick to accept the blame. 'No, the fault was entirely mine. On your lead of the ◇2 I can place you with a diamond honour. Whether it is the King or the Jack, it costs me nothing to play the ◇Q at trick one. The crucial difference is that I could then put you on play with the ◇J to secure the killing spade switch.'

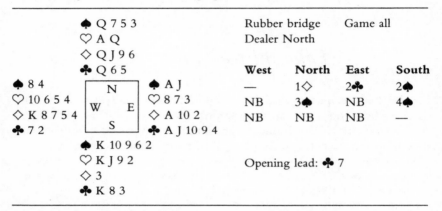

	♠ Q 7 5 3		
	♡ A Q	Rubber bridge	Game all
	◇ Q J 9 6	Dealer North	
	♣ Q 6 5		

	West	North	East	South
♠ 8 4 / N W E S / ♠ A J	—	1◇	2♣	2♠
♡ 10 6 5 4 / ♡ 8 7 3	NB	3♠	NB	4♠
◇ K 8 7 5 4 / ◇ A 10 2	NB	NB	NB	—
♣ 7 2 / ♣ A J 10 9 4				

	♠ K 10 9 6 2	
	♡ K J 9 2	Opening lead: ♣ 7
	◇ 3	
	♣ K 8 3	

At trick one East played the ♣9 which lost to declarer's ♣K. Aware of the impending club ruff, declarer played three rounds of hearts, discarding a club from dummy, before continuing with a second club. East won the ♣A and made the good play of the ♣J, which West ruffed with the ♠8, forcing dummy to overruff with the ♠Q. When declarer played a small spade from dummy the stage was set for East to complete a capable defence. All he has to do is win with the ♠A and put his partner on play with the ◇K. West plays a heart and East's ♠J scores the setting trick. Unhappily, East took the ♠A and cashed the ◇A. There was no second chance.

'If only you had petered in hearts, I would have played a small diamond', East bleated.

'What could you lose,' West asked, 'by playing a low diamond anyway, except an insignificant overtrick?'

Both these errors stem from the same cause, a failure to concentrate on the simple fact that to defeat a major suit game, you must win four tricks, not three.

Beyond the book

A table of recommended opening leads seems to be an essential ingredient of most elementary bridge books. The list invariably starts with the blue-blooded **AKQ** and **KQJ** and finishes with the proletarian **Jxx** and lowly **xxx**.

The absurd rigidity of this tuition reminds me of an incident in my school cadet corps. As a necessary preliminary to field day manoeuvres, we filed into the armoury to collect our kit from the Quartermaster Sergeant. When it came to my turn, he gravely handed me a large cylindrical block of wood, attached to a leather sling.

'What is that supposed to be?', I asked.

'Have you no imagination, Lance Corporal? It is a *trench mortar.*'

Swiftly calculating that carrying this clumsy object as I tramped five miles over ploughed fields would make the day even more wearisome, I made what I thought was a helpful offer.

'Sergeant Major, I am prepared to *imagine* that I am carrying a deadly weapon, without any constant physical reminder.'

The old trooper bristled. 'One day', he barked, 'you will learn the value of discipline and unquestioning obedience'.

At the bridge table, and probably in today's army, blind adherence to a set of rules is a poor substitute for logical thought.

The first decision that the opening leader must make is strategical. Should he attack, or play passive? Only when he has made up his mind should he then decide which suit and which card offer the best chance of fulfilling his tactical objective. The text books say that it is correct to attack when leading against a small slam, but to play safe against a grand slam. Suppose you hold this hand as West:

♠ K 8 4
♡ K 8 4
♢ K 2
♣ J 10 8 7 6

The opponents have bid as follows:

South	North
1 ♠	2 NT
3 ♡	4 ♣
4 ♢	5 ♣
5 ♡	6 ♡
NB	—

To select an attacking lead would be insanity. The bidding suggests that the opponents have little to spare, and that your two major Kings may represent an unsurmountable stumbling block. But change the bidding sequence:

South	North
1 ♠	3 ◇
3 ♠	4 ♠
5 ♣	5 ◇
6 ♠	NB

Now your ◇K has become a liability rather than an asset. Left in peace, declarer will probably lose a trick to your ♠K, and then develop the diamonds with the help of a successful finesse. This is the time to *attack*. Lead a heart.

'Lead the fourth highest of your longest and strongest suit against no trumps' is a further piece of advice that does not deserve uncritical compliance. Consider this hand.

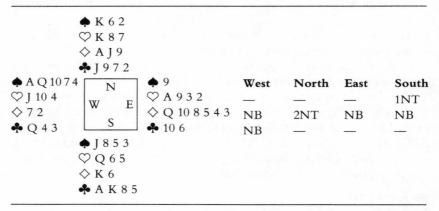

```
            ♠ K 6 2
            ♡ K 8 7
            ◇ A J 9
            ♣ J 9 7 2
♠ A Q 10 7 4   ┌─────┐   ♠ 9
♡ J 10 4       │  N  │   ♡ A 9 3 2
◇ 7 2          │ W E │   ◇ Q 10 8 5 4 3
♣ Q 4 3        │  S  │   ♣ 10 6
            └─────┘
            ♠ J 8 5 3
            ♡ Q 6 5
            ◇ K 6
            ♣ A K 8 5
```

West	North	East	South
—	—	—	1NT
NB	2NT	NB	NB
NB	—	—	—

You are West.

On your lead of a small spade, a capable declarer will make eight tricks. Winning the spade lead in hand he will dislodge your ♣Q. When you astutely switch to the ♡J, he will rise with dummy's ♡K, limiting the defence to two heart tricks. The defenders no longer possess the communications to take more than five tricks.

Study the effect of the opening lead of the ♡J. Declarer, deprived of the present of a trick on the lead, will fight a losing battle to establish his eighth trick.

Of course, it is unfortunate that East has a singleton spade, but the point is more fundamental. Against 3NT it is sometimes good business to sacrifice the trick for the tempo. Against 2NT the defence will often have time to change direction. A generalization with some merit is that it is right to attack against 3NT but prefer more passive openings against no trump part scores.

The interior sequence is another worthy target for the aspiring iconoclast.

| | ♠ Q 9 7 2 | | Rubber bridge | Game all |
| | ♡ K Q 10 4 | | Dealer South | |

```
              ♠ Q 9 7 2
              ♡ K Q 10 4
              ◇ 9 8
              ♣ K Q 10
♠ A J 10 6 5    N       ♠ 8 4
♡ 7 2        W     E    ♡ J 9 5 3
◇ A J 2         S       ◇ 7 5 3
♣ 9 8 7                 ♣ A 4 3 2
              ♠ K 3
              ♡ A 8 6
              ◇ K Q 10 6 4
              ♣ J 6 5
```

Rubber bridge — Game all
Dealer South

West	North	East	South
—	—	—	1NT
NB	2♣	NB	2◇
NB	3NT	NB	NB
NB	—	—	—

Opening lead: ♠ J

Encouraged by his two tens, North stretches for game. The destiny of the contract is soon decided. Declarer allows the ♠J to run to his ♠K. He then crosses to dummy with the ♡Q in order to play a diamond towards his hand. West is powerless. He cannot prevent declarer from establishing his diamonds, because dummy's ♠9 provides a crucial third spade stop. If West had selected the ♠6 for his opening lead, it would have been a very different story. When he obtains the lead, West can cash the ♠A and use his equals to dislodge dummy's ♠Q.

When to switch

A defender who obtains the lead early in the defence against three no trumps will often face a difficult and critical decision. Should he persevere with the suit that his partner has led, or should he switch? Even when it is obvious that he must switch, the choice of suit or the selection of the actual card may be far from self-evident.

Beginners are usually taught 'return your partner's suit' as a rule of thumb. With a little experience they will soon learn that the exceptions are so frequent that the 'rule' must be observed with discretion. It does,

141

however, possess one psychological advantage. In my experience, partners tend to be forgiving if you do not find a killing switch, infinitely less so if you fail to return their suit which they have carefully established.

As we shall see, this is a problem which players of all standards find perplexing. In my first example, East was no beginner.

```
              ♠ A K Q 8 3
              ♡ A J 9 2
              ◇ 10 7
              ♣ 6 2
  ♠ 6 5                        ♠ 10 9 4 2
  ♡ 7 6 5 3       N            ♡ K Q 4
  ◇ A 5 2     W     E          ◇ Q 9 8 4
  ♣ K Q 8 5       S            ♣ 10 9
              ♠ J 7
              ♡ 10 8
              ◇ K J 6 3
              ♣ A J 7 4 3
```

Rubber bridge   Game all
Dealer North

West	North	East	South
—	1♠	NB	2♣
NB	2♡	NB	2NT
NB	3NT	NB	NB
NB	—	—	—

Opening lead: ♡ 7

Declarer played low from dummy on West's excellent opening lead, permitting East to win with the ♡Q. East switched to the ◇4 on which South played small and West was obliged to win with the ◇A. The defence had missed its chance.

The train of thought which should have prompted East to find the club switch turns on West's probable distribution. If he had four diamonds he might well have preferred the lead of the unbid suit to the theoretically dangerous lead of dummy's second suit. Furthermore, if West had had the magical ◇AJx, East would probably have another chance when he regained the lead with the ♡K.

The next hand occurred in the round robin of the Bermuda Bowl in 1971. Both France and the American Aces reached three no trumps by an identical bidding sequence. We study the events in the closed room, where the contract was made.

		East-West game
♠ 9 7		Dealer South
♡ K 9 5 3		**Closed room**
◇ 8 7		
♣ A 10 9 7 5		

♠ K 6 4	N	♠ Q 10 8 2
♡ Q 6 2	W E	♡ J 10 8
◇ Q 10 9 2	S	◇ K 6 4
♣ Q J 4		♣ 8 6 3

♠ A J 5 3	
♡ A 7 4	
◇ A J 5 3	
♣ K 2	

West	North	East	South
Hamman	*Svarc*	*Eisenberg*	*Boulenger*
—	—	—	1NT
NB	2♣	NB	2♠
NB	2NT	NB	3NT
NB	NB	NB	—

Opening lead: ◇ 9

Eisenberg was allowed to win the first trick with the ◇K. The lead of the nine promised either two or no higher honours, in this case obviously the former. Not unnaturally, he continued with the ◇6. It may seem harsh to criticize, but I believe there were two clues which might have suggested to a player of Eisenberg's brilliance that the diamond return was wrong.

At the table he would doubtless have known that declarer had the ◇AJ. With the ◇AJx, declarer will usually win the first round, unless he can ensure that the defender with the length in the suit will not obtain the lead when the suit is established. If Eisenberg had reasoned that declarer had four diamonds, then the small cards assume an ominous significance. As Eisenberg's second highest diamond was the six, dummy's ◇8 would prevent West from clearing the suit. Even if Eisenberg had recognized the need to switch, he would still have had to decide on the right suit and the correct card. No doubt he would have chosen spades, and for him the selection of the ♠10 would have been routine.

In the open room, declarer took the ◇A at trick one. Three rounds of clubs found West on play. Jean-Marc Roudinesco, for France, did well to find the spade switch. Declarer put the defence to two awkward discards on the long clubs. Roudinesco parted with a diamond and a spade. Declarer continued with two rounds of hearts, on the second of which Roudinesco followed with the ♡Q.

It is not surprising that declarer should have misread the distribution. He exited with the ♠J, successfully putting West on play. But Roudinesco, who had bared the ♠K, completed a beautiful defence by meanly producing the ♡6, to defeat the contract by two tricks.

To say that a defender faces a difficult decision, but offer no concrete advice, is singularly unhelpful. Even if there is no all-embracing rule or principle, a good defender will always think along the following lines before committing himself. From the bidding and the opening lead he will try to picture the distribution of the unseen hands. Where declarer has made a limit bid, he will form an accurate assessment of the strength of his partner's hand. If declarer's hand is unlimited, he will be forced to make an assumption of the high cards which his partner must hold if the defence is to succeed. He will take careful note of any clues which emerge from declarer's line of play.

Sometimes it will be clear that a switch is either imperative or doomed to failure. More often a player will be forced to rely on the one indispensable quality of the good bridge player, judgement.

A lesson for the upper fifth

Beginners are invariably taught to avoid giving declarer a ruff and discard. If they persist with their studies they will learn, perhaps with some surprise, that there are a number of distinct settings in which the only hope for the defence lies in the deliberate concession of a ruff and discard. I shall discuss three of them.

This hand illustrates a well worn theme much loved by bridge writers:

	♠ A 2		
	♡ A Q 7 4 3		
	◇ A 9 4 2		
	♣ K 3		

Rubber bridge   Game all
Dealer South

♠ K 10 8 7 3   ♠ Q J 6 5
♡ 2   ♡ 6 5
◇ 8 6 5   ◇ Q 3
♣ Q J 10 9   ♣ 8 7 6 5 4

♠ 9 4
♡ K J 10 9 8
◇ K J 10 7
♣ A 2

West	North	East	South
—	—	—	1♡
NB	4NT	NB	5◇
NB	5NT	NB	6♡
NB	NB	NB	—

Opening lead: ♣ Q

North, no admirer of delicate approach bidding, has effectively raised South's opening bid of one heart to six hearts, fortified by the largely irrelevant knowledge that South has one Ace.

West leads the ♣Q, declarer wins the lead in hand, draws trumps in two rounds, and plays dummy's ♣K. Then he cashes the ♠A and continues with a second round of spades. It does not matter which defender wins the trick, the problem is identical. Declarer has to find the $\diamond$Q. Unless the defence plays diamonds, declarer will have to rely on guesswork. By counting, both defenders should appreciate that the ruff and discard will be of no assistance whatsoever to declarer, whereas to open up the diamond suit could be fatal.

In my second example, East saw the best chance for the defence.

```
              ♠ K Q 8
              ♡ A K Q 6 5
              ◇ A K Q
              ♣ Q 3
♠ A 5         ┌─────────┐      ♠ J 5 4
♡ 8 3         │    N    │      ♡ 9 4 2
◇ J 8 7       │  W   E  │      ◇ 6 5 3 2
♣ A K 10 9 7 6│    S    │      ♣ 8 5 4
              └─────────┘
              ♠ 10 9 7 6 2
              ♡ J 10 7
              ◇ 10 9 4
              ♣ J 2
```

Teams   Game all
Dealer North

West	North	East	South
—	2♣	NB	2◇
NB	2♡	NB	2♠
NB	3♣	NB	4♠
NB	NB	NB	—

Opening lead: ♣ K

West cashes the two top clubs, on which East contributes the ♣4 and ♣5. Pausing to consider, West sees that the only chance for the defence must lie in the establishment of a second trump trick. Accordingly, West continues with a third round of clubs, offering a ruff and discard. Declarer ruffs in hand, and plays a spade, which West wins with the ♠A. West completes the long range promotion by continuing with a fourth round of clubs. Whatever declarer does, East's ♠J is promoted to score the setting trick.

My final hand turns on a different point:

```
              ♠ A Q 7 4
              ♡ K Q 10 8 7
              ◇ 4 3
              ♣ 5 2
♠ 8 3         ┌─────────┐      ♠ 6 5 2
♡ 9 2         │    N    │      ♡ A J 5 3
◇ A J 5 2     │  W   E  │      ◇ 8 6
♣ K Q 10 7 4  │    S    │      ♣ J 9 6 3
              └─────────┘
              ♠ K J 10 9
              ♡ 6 4
              ◇ K Q 10 9 7
              ♣ A 8
```

Pairs   Game all
Dealer South

West	North	East	South
—	—	—	1◇
NB	1♡	NB	1♠
NB	4♠	NB	NB
NB	—	—	—

Opening lead: ♣ K

Declarer wins the club lead in hand. Relying on the superficial analysis that there are only three losers, he mistakenly draws three rounds of trumps, finishing in dummy. He continues with a diamond to the ◇Q, which West ducks. Now declarer plays a heart to the ♡K, which East allows to win, and a second round of diamonds on which declarer's ◇10 loses to West's ◇J. West switches to hearts and declarer, appreciating that West is unlikely to hold the Ace, plays dummy's ♡10, which loses to East's ♡J. The defence have taken two tricks. East cashes the ♣J and continues with a third round of clubs conceding a ruff and discard, which is of no use to declarer. Whichever hand takes the ruff, declarer will be bereft of entries, even though a ruffing finesse would establish either red suit. Declarer is held to eight tricks.

If the defence had continued either red suit, he would have made his contract. Although it was a mistake to draw trumps, a less expert defence would have permitted the error to go unpunished. Admittedly, withholding the red aces was a weakening preliminary, but the ruff and discard was the mortal thrust.

Never again . . .

'Never' and 'always' are words that should be used sparingly when discussing bridge. Blind acceptance of dogma is the unmistakable signature tune of the moderate player. Nevertheless I have one inflexible rule: 'Never double a part score with only two trumps.'

The last time I broke my rule was more than two years ago, but the memory is still painful. The hand below is an echo of that experience.

	♠ 9 8 7		
	♡ 7 2		
	◇ 8 4		
	♣ 10 9 7 4 3 2		

Rubber bridge East–West game
Dealer East

♠ 6 5   ♠ Q 10 4 3
♡ K 10 8 6 5 3   ♡ Q J 9
◇ J 10 6 2   ◇ K Q 9 7
♣ J   ♣ Q 6

West	North	East	South
—	—	1NT	Dble
2♡	NB	NB	Dble
NB	NB	NB	—

♠ A K J 2
♡ A 4
◇ A 5 3
♣ A K 8 5

Opening lead: ♡ 7

East-West were playing a weak no trump. Understandably South thought that his hand gave him a marvellous opportunity to expose the folly of the system. He was to be disappointed.

The contract could have been defeated by a diamond ruff, but North reasonably chose the ♡7 as his opening lead, which cost the defence a vital tempo. As North-South could make 11 tricks in clubs or in no trumps, a penalty of 200 from two hearts doubled would have been poor compensation. Some critics would blame North for accepting the double, but in my opinion the criticism would be ill founded. South's double is a penalty double, showing a strong hand with some strength in hearts. On that basis it is a bad mistake to double for penalties at the two level with only two trumps.

I have said that 'never' and 'always' should be used sparingly, but here 'always' is appropriate:

West	North	East	South
1♡	Dbl	NB	NB
NB	—	—	—

When an informatory double at the one level is transposed into a penalty double by a pass it is invariably correct for North to lead a trump. To justify the penalty pass South's trumps should, ideally, be sequential. The winning defence is to draw trumps. A trump lead may enable South to do so.

Again, when the opponents have bid and supported a suit which your partner has doubled for penalties at a low level it is usually correct to lead a trump.

If your side obviously possesses the majority of the high cards, but the opponents stubbornly continue bidding, a trump lead will normally be the one to exact the maximum penalty. Whenever the opponents rely exclusively on the power of their trumps, draw them, and you remove the sting from the adder.

Here is a striking example:

```
          ♠ 8 7
          ♡ 2
          ◇ 9 7 4 2
          ♣ Q 10 8 7 6 5
♠ A Q J 2  ┌─────────┐  ♠ 9 6 5 4
♡ J 4 3    │    N    │  ♡ K 9 8 5
◇ K J 3    │  W   E  │  ◇ 8
♣ A K J    │    S    │  ♣ 9 4 3 2
           └─────────┘
          ♠ K 10 3
          ♡ A Q 10 7 6
          ◇ A Q 10 6 5
          ♣ Void
```

Rubber bridge East–West game+40
Dealer West

West	North	East	South
2NT	NB	NB	3♡
NB	NB	Dble	NB
NB	4♣	Dble	4◇
Dble	NB	NB	NB

Opening lead: ♣ K

The bidding was typical of those rubber bridge schools in which players rescue their partners for no good reason. It was infuriating for East–West to find that their opponents had undeservedly stumbled into their best contract.

West was the celebrated chess international Richard Newman, who has now successfully transferred his talents to bridge. Describing this exasperating hand, he said: 'I know only too well that on this sort of bidding one should lead a trump to cut down the cross ruff, but with ◇KJ3 I lacked the courage. I then had the mortification of watching declarer waltz from hand to hand, finishing with ten tricks.'

Few players would be so self-critical.

Close analysis reveals that the lead of the small diamond is not good enough. Suppose declarer wins the opening lead in dummy with the ◇9, he can take the heart finesse, cash the ♡A, discarding a spade, and ruff a heart in dummy. He returns to hand with a club ruff and plays a fourth round of hearts. It is immaterial whether West ruffs or discards. Dummy's fourth trump will enable declarer to score his tenth trick.

Does that mean that there is no lead which defeats four diamonds, doubled? No. Curiously, only the sparkling lead of a trump honour deprives declarer of the vital early entry which he needs to take the heart finesse. I wonder if overlooking that opening lead will cause Newman to wear his hair shirt.

SEVEN

The telescope, the stethoscope and a look over your shoulder

Bridge, like wine, is a living organism, changing all the time. Some of the developments have undoubtedly enriched the game. Even those violently opposed to artificial systems would surely concede that the Italian influence has taken bridge into a different dimension. But equally it must be admitted that the increasing complexity of the game is one of the reasons why rubber bridge players are reluctant to try their hand at duplicate. Another deterrent is the brash manners of some experienced players who should know better.

Bridge as currently shown on television may be imperfect, but it is a gigantic step forward towards popularising the game. Some sponsors may still think that bridge does not provide a sufficiently exciting image to market their wares. Luckily, others are more enlightened.

I seem to remember dimly from my school days that a knowledge of history is supposed to enable one to foresee and better understand the problems of the future. To look backwards in bridge provides a valuable yardstick for judging whether modern innovations have produced real improvement or only unnecessary complications.

Outlook rough

'I am disenchanted with tournament bridge'.

The speaker was not, as you might suppose, a venerable international. He was one of Britain's best young players.

'The trouble is the lack of competition against top class opposition', he continued. 'In the normal season you might play one match against a good team and possibly a Camrose match. The rest of the time is spent in rabbit killing, where even victory is unfulfilling.'

Sadly, this sense of frustration is shared by other good young players. The administrators of the English Bridge Union are a devoted body of men who generously give their time to the myriad of different problems inherent in controlling an amateur game. Very reasonably they have directed their principal efforts to the cultivation of the grass roots. This admirable horticultural policy can only be criticized if it results in the total neglect of the 'flowers that bloom in the spring, tra la'.

British bridge stands at the cross roads, with the very considerable danger that it might select the 'no through road'. In 1960 it was truthfully said that Britain could select any of four teams, all capable of achieving distinction at a European Championship. Today it is hard to find *one*, and the results since 1976 seem to confirm the decline. For those who refuse to accept that Britain is no longer a major bridge power, the warnings are surely too clear to ignore.

I believe that the solution lies in the creation of a two–tier system. Leave the local congresses and county championships as they are. By all means preserve those charming social anachronisms, the Hubert Phillips Bowl and the Portland Pairs. It is the major competitions which require an urgent reappraisal. Not many years ago, the leading experts played in all the major competitions. Today many of the big names are missing, which is not merely complacency on the part of the experts. I believe that major competitions could be revitalized by sponsorship, so that they attract the participation of the rising stars and the leading players who retain any international aspirations. Many sports organizers have recognized that sponsorship is essential if their championships are not to lose their lustre. Bridge players should not be too proud to emulate them.

The London County Contract Bridge Association stages the Richard Lederer Memorial Trophy, one of the very few master events in the calendar. The holders, C. Dixon, V. Silverstone, E. Martin, G. Calder-wood, P. Alder and P. Jourdain, retained the trophy from a field which bristled with former world and European champions. Victor Silverstone, with fellow-Scotsman Willie Coyle, was a constant thistle in

150

the side of English Camrose teams. Silverstone has moved South, where he has struck up an equally fine partnership with Chris Dixon, who represented Great Britain in Athens and Miami. In addition to winning the trophy, Silverstone won not only the award for the best played hand, but also the award for the best defended hand. Here he is as declarer.

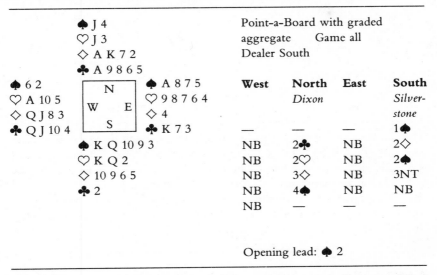

	♠ J 4		Point-a-Board with graded
	♡ J 3		aggregate Game all
	♢ A K 7 2		Dealer South
	♣ A 9 8 6 5		

		♠ A 8 7 5		West	North	East	South
♠ 6 2		♡ 9 8 7 6 4			Dixon		Silver-
♡ A 10 5	N / W E / S	♢ 4					stone
♢ Q J 8 3		♣ K 7 3					
♣ Q J 10 4				—	—	—	1♠
	♠ K Q 10 9 3			NB	2♣	NB	2♢
	♡ K Q 2			NB	2♡	NB	2♠
	♢ 10 9 6 5			NB	3♢	NB	3NT
	♣ 2			NB	4♠	NB	NB
				NB	—	—	—

Opening lead: ♠ 2

Silverstone's vulnerable opening bid would not receive the unqualified approval of conservative critics. However, it was a sure-footed auction, ending with a well judged four spades from Dixon.

East permitted declarer to win the trump lead in hand. Silverstone played a heart and when dummy's ♡J won, continued with a second heart which West won, returning a third heart. Silverstone played a spade to dummy's ♠J, which East unwisely took with the ♠A in order to continue with a fourth round of hearts, forcing Silverstone to ruff. West discarded a club. When declarer drew the remaining trumps, West parted with the ♣10 and ♣J. Reading West's distribution accurately, Silverstone crossed to dummy with the ♢A, cashed the ♣A, and played the ♢2 to his ♢9 and West's ♢J. With nothing to play but diamonds, West's two apparently certain diamond tricks were reduced to one.

The bidding on the second hand from the same tournament, demonstrates that the experts, who shall be nameless, are fallible.

♠ A 7 6 4
♡ J 8 3
♢ 8 4 3 2
♣ 10 2

```
    N
W       E
    S
```

♠ K J 9 8 3
♡ A K Q 10 7 6
♢ A
♣ Q

Game all
Dealer East

West	North	East	South
—	—	1♢	Dble
NB	1♠	NB	2♢
NB	2NT	NB	3♢
NB	3♡	NB	4♣
NB	4♢	NB	4♡
NB	NB	NB	—

The baffling intricacy of this sequence would have done credit to the librettist of *Cosi Fan Tutti*. To be fair to North it is always difficult to find the right bid on a weak hand when your partner will not let you off the hook, but four diamonds was the cry of a drowning man. As East had ♠Q5, declarer made twelve tricks. Aware of the renown of their opponents at the other table North-South anticipated a heavy loss. Little did they know. This was the auction:

West	North	East	South
—	—	1♢	1♡
NB	NB	NB	—

So instead of losing 13 IMPs, they gained 10 IMPs. I am reliably informed that the post-mortem at the second table was less abbreviated than the bidding sequence.

The best hand for ages

The age at which a bridge player reaches his peak remains debatable. Before expressing any opinion, let me introduce as evidence a hand which was first reported by Alan Truscott in *The New York Times*.

```
                ♠ A K Q 5 4          Teams      Love all
                ♡ 10 6 2            Dealer South
                ◇ 7
                ♣ Q 8 5 3
♠ J 10 9 7 6 2  ┌─────┐  ♠ 8 3
♡ Q             │  N  │  ♡ K 4
◇ A Q 10 4      │W   E│  ◇ J 9 8 6 2
♣ 7 2           │  S  │  ♣ A J 10 9
                └─────┘
                ♠ Void
                ♡ A J 9 8 7 5 3
                ◇ K 5 3
                ♣ K 6 4
```

West	North	East	South
—	—	—	1♡
1♠	2♠	NB	3♡
NB	4♡	NB	NB
NB	—	—	—

Opening lead: ♣ 7

North's bid of two spades would not be everyone's choice, but no call is entirely satisfactory. A penalty double would be an inferior alternative, because despite the AKQ, the spade suit lacks the requisite texture.

Declarer instantly recognized his problem, the lack of a quick entry to dummy. He made his first good decision when he played dummy's ♣Q. East took the ♣A and returned the suit, declarer winning with the ♣K. The play of the ♣Q had disrupted the defence's communications in the club suit. To minimize the chance of East regaining the lead, declarer continued with the ◇K, West took the ◇A but the defence could not prevent declarer obtaining a club discard on dummy's top spades. Undoubtedly a fine example of the expert touch by the declarer, Dougie Hsieh. Hsieh became an American life master at exactly 11 years, 10 months, and 4 days old. The next hand occurred at rubber bridge.

```
                ♠ K J 4             North-South game
                ♡ K 9 3 2          Dealer South
                ◇ 10 4
                ♣ 10 8 4 2
♠ Q 10 9 7 6    ┌─────┐  ♠ 3 2
♡ Void          │  N  │  ♡ J 8 7 6
◇ K Q 5 3       │W   E│  ◇ J 9 2
♣ A K 9 3       │  S  │  ♣ Q J 7 6
                └─────┘
                ♠ A 8 5
                ♡ A Q 10 5 4
                ◇ A 8 7 6
                ♣ 5
```

West	North	East	South
—	—	—	1♡
Dble	Redble	NB	NB
1♠	2♡	NB	4♡
NB	NB	NB	—

Opening lead: ♣ K

North would have been wiser to bid three hearts rather than redouble, although with the spades marked on the left the final contract was an excellent one. On the first trick East unwisely played the ♣Q, and West compliantly continued with the ♣3, covered by dummy's ♣8 and West's ♣J, which declarer ruffed.

The play of the ♡A revealed the bad trump break, which meant that it was no longer possible to make ten tricks by a straightforward line. Declarer played a low diamond to dummy's ♢10 and East's ♢J. If East had returned a club, declarer could have succeeded by discarding a losing diamond but East's return of a trump was less accommodating. Declarer won in hand with the ♡10, cashed the ♠A, successfully finessed the ♠J, and played the ♠K, ruffed by East. This was the five-card ending:

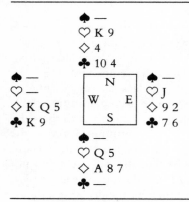

East recognized that the return of a club or a diamond would enable declarer to make the remainder of the tricks on a cross-ruff, so he played the ♡J. When declarer covered with the ♡Q West found himself in the revolving doors of an overtaking squeeze. If he discards a diamond, declarer can establish the long diamond with one ruff, and if he discards a club, declarer overtakes the ♡Q with dummy's ♡K and establishes dummy's ♣10 by ruffing a club in hand.

The declarer was Louis Ellison, a leading expert in the mid-1950s who, although he does not look it, is now over 80.

Superficially the 'evidence' seems inconclusive, but we have only examined technique. The bridge expert needs time to acquire maturity of judgement and experience. On the other side of the coin, both stamina and concentration decline with age. At 50, some players obstinately refuse to recognize the undeniable merits of some technical innovations. Others develop personal whims or quirks.

Naturally, I remain immune from such foibles, even if I do refuse to sit with my back to the room, or lend anyone my pen.

Making a strong pass

As some of my articles describe the events of years gone by, I shall try to redress the balance by looking through the other end of the telescope.

What does the future hold for bridge? Of one thing I am certain; bridge, whether as a family entertainment or in the field of international competition, will remain vibrantly alive. Unlike games which merely enjoy a passing vogue, bridge has unlimited variety and is complex enough to resist the efforts of any player to become its absolute master.

It has been said that bridge is not suitable for television because it is not a spectator sport. I believe that is an overstatement. In the past, people have flocked to watch the game when the personalities were colourful or the issues at stake were sufficiently provocative. It is hardly surprising that the public displays no enthusiasm for watching anaemic struggles for minor trophies. Possibly more than any other game, bridge has to be well presented. Whereas the significance of potting the black, or scoring a triple 20 at darts, is instantly apparent, bridge unfortunately does demand some previous knowledge of the game if one is to watch it with interest.

When the right formula is found to project bridge on television, I am confident that the programmes will attract a more committed audience than the games which depend upon their instant appeal.

Another development that I foresee is that more players will adopt the 'strong pass' system. For those who hate complicated artificial bidding, there is temporary good news. Britain and some other countries have banned the system in domestic competition, so for the moment Frankenstein's creation remains safely locked in a foreign castle.

The basic idea of the system is very simple. With any hand strong enough to open the bidding if you were playing an orthodox system, you 'pass' as dealer or second to speak. The corollary is that all other bids are released to describe sub-minimum hands. Opposite a partner who has passed, you are *obliged* to open the bidding. Undoubtedly the system increases the bidding vocabulary. At a recent European tournament the bidding was: pass, pass, pass, pass.

What is interesting about that, you may ask. Apparently *both* pairs were playing the strong pass system, so that the players who passed in third and fourth position were in breach of their 'marriage vows'. There were protests and counter protests, and the incident opened up untilled land for the law givers.

My final prediction envisages the greater use of computers. At the World Bridge Olympiad in Valkenberg a computer was programmed to bid according to Benito Garozzo's Volmac system. The machine's bidding was shown alongside the human bidding on Bridgerama, which gave an amusing comparison. Sensibly, the programmers recognized that competitive bidding would give the poor thing mechanical indigestion — so its activities were wisely restricted to free run auctions.

When Sweden played against Holland, the computer was in good form.

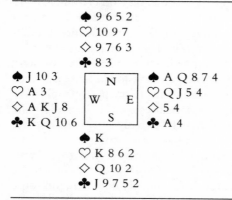

```
                ♠ 9 6 5 2
                ♡ 10 9 7
                ♢ 9 7 6 3
                ♣ 8 3
♠ J 10 3                        ♠ A Q 8 7 4
♡ A 3           N              ♡ Q J 5 4
♢ A K J 8    W     E           ♢ 5 4
♣ K Q 10 6      S              ♣ A 4
                ♠ K
                ♡ K 8 6 2
                ♢ Q 10 2
                ♣ J 9 7 5 2
```

Sweden bid well to reach the excellent spade slam. This was the Dutch sequence:

West	East
Vergoed	*Kreijns*
1 ♣	1 ♠
2 ♢	2 ♡
2 ♠	3 ♣
3 NT	NB

Garozzo coached both the Dutch open and ladies team. It was ironic to find his computer outbidding his pupils as it did here.

West	East
1 ♣	1 ♠
1 NT	2 ♡
2 ♠	3 ♣
3 ♢	3 ♡
4 ♠	5 ♣
5 ♢	5 ♠
6 ♠	NB

The bidding followed the relay principle, with West asking questions and East describing his hand. West learned that East had five spades and four hearts and four controls (an ace = 2, a king = 1). Five clubs promised extra values, in this case the ♠Q and the ♡Q J. This information enabled West to bid the slam.

On the next hand, the computer outbid both its human counterparts.

West	East
♠ K Q 10 2	♠ J 7 5
♡ Q 9 7 4	♡ K 10 6
◇ A Q 6	◇ J 10 9 7 5
♣ Q 8	♣ K 2

This was the way the Swedes bid:

West	East
1 NT	2 ♣
2 ♡	2 NT

With the duplicated weakness in clubs, declarer was defeated by three tricks.
This was the Dutch sequence:

West	East
1 NT	3 NT

The Dutch made a trick more in the play — so there was no swing.
The computer showed fine judgement when it bid:

West	East
1 ◇	1 NT
2 ♡	NB

One diamond showed one of many things, but guaranteed 11-15 points. East's response denied a four card major and promised 7-11 points. West's rebid said I have a maximum hand with four cards in both majors. There is no doubt that a part score in either major is an improvement on two or three no trumps.

While Volmac was performing in Valkenburg, my friend Victor Mollo was doing battle with another genus of the species, the 'brain chip' of Fidelity Electronics in London. Mollo had been highly sceptical of the manufacturer's claims for its 'superb playing skill' and had issued a challenge. For a while the gauntlet was ignored, but sportingly confound ing the cynics the British distributors eventually agreed to a rubber bridge match of 32 hands for high stakes and a case of vintage champagne.

When I asked him who won, Mollo cryptically replied, 'We all did. My partner Derek Rimington and I won the money and the champagne which you are tasting, but the computer demonstrated that even if it lacked the skill to win a world championship, it was quite capable of playing with the average player, and that, after all, is the role for which it was primarily designed.'

'Do you feel equally confident of victory against a more sophisticated version?' I asked.

Mollo paused. 'What do you think of the champagne?' he parried.

'Excellent — the computer evidently has good taste', I replied.

'Exactly', said Mollo, with a twinkle. 'A very good reason to give the computer its revenge.'

All-time tops

This is the time of year when the weather forces sports writers to compose teams of players from different generations. With less excuse, I shall permit myself a similar indulgence.

It is nearly 40 years since the European Bridge Championships were resumed after the Second World War. Taking as the criterion that a player's ability is assessed at the height of his powers, who would be the 10 strongest players to represent Great Britain? With the caveat of the old penny slot machine, 'for amusement only', here is my list:

1. J.T. Reese
2. M. Harrison Gray
3. J. Cansino
4. A. Meredith
5. B. Schapiro
6. R.A. Priday
   C. Rodrigue
8. N. Gardener
9. R. Sheehan
10. K. Konstam

Few would dispute that Reese's unerring accuracy entitles him to be considered primus inter pares. Harrison Gray died in 1968, but even in his last years he still retained an extraordinary grasp of the game. This is a hand that he played many years ago.

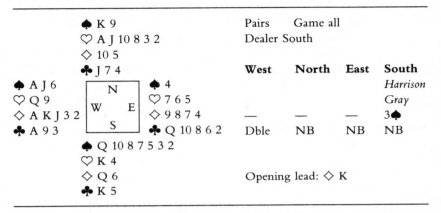

		Pairs	Game all
		Dealer South	

♠ K 9
♡ A J 10 8 3 2
♢ 10 5
♣ J 7 4

	West	North	East	South
				Harrison
				Gray

♠ A J 6   ♠ 4
♡ Q 9   ♡ 7 6 5
♢ A K J 3 2   ♢ 9 8 7 4
♣ A 9 3   ♣ Q 10 8 6 2

West	North	East	South
—	—	—	3♠
Dble	NB	NB	NB

♠ Q 10 8 7 5 3 2
♡ K 4
♢ Q 6
♣ K 5

Opening lead: ♢ K

West played the ♢K and ♢A, and switched to the ♣A, on which East after reflection played the ♣8. West continued with a second club on which Gray craftily played dummy's ♣J which was covered by East's ♣Q. The fate of the hand hung on whether he could find the ♠J. From West's penalty double, Gray was almost certain that he must hold ♠AJx, but he preferred absolute certainties. Before playing a spade, *he cashed the* ♡K. With the skill of a practised illusionist he created the impression that he was trying to enter dummy to discard his losing club on the ♡A. When Gray played a spade, West swallowed the bait and took the ♠A at once.

I might be criticized for favouring the players who dominated the 1970s. But many good judges, including the Italian Blue team, insist that had Cansino enjoyed better health he would have been recognized as one of the great players of all time. To resist the criticism on more general grounds, it must be acknowledged that championship bridge has grown increasingly complicated. Although it may not be necessary to play a complex codified system oneself, it is essential to understand the mechanics of one's opponents' methods, and the inferences which arise from them. I do not suggest that the older players would be incapable of unravelling the new systems, merely that their established supremacy appeared less absolute against the artificial systems.

Remarkably, Nico Gardener has not represented Great Britain since 1961, yet he still retains his flawless technique. Gardener is above all an elegant stylist. He would deplore the modern players who slam the cards on the table in order to underline their reputation for aggression. When he plays a card, he does so with the polite menace with which one imagines Mephistopheles might have presented his visiting card to Faust.

This hand illustrates his well earned reputation for prescience.

	♠ 7 4 2			
	♡ 6 3			
	◇ A K 8 5 3 2		Teams of four	Game all
	♣ Q 6		Dealer East	

	West	North	East	South
♠ 9 8 3 / ♠ A Q 6 5				*Gardener*
♡ A 9 8 / ♡ 10 4				
◇ Q 9 7 4 / ◇ J 10	—	—	1♣	1♡
♣ J 10 5 / ♣ A K 9 3 2	1NT	2◇	2♠	3♡
	NB	NB	NB	—

South hand:
- ♠ K J 10
- ♡ K Q J 7 5 2
- ◇ 6
- ♣ 8 7 4

Opening lead: ♣ J

East took the opening lead with the ♣K and cashed the ♣A. He continued with the ♠A and ♠5. The hand looks deceptively simple. Most players would win with the ♠K, ruff a club in dummy, cash the ◇AK discarding a spade, and hope to lose only the Ace of trumps. Looking at all four hands, it is not difficult to see what would happen. When West obtains the lead with the ♡A, he plays a diamond which East ruffs with the ♡10. The upper-cut neatly promotes West's ♡9 to provide a second trump trick for the defence.

Gardener did not play the ♠K, he finessed the ♠10. After he had ruffed a club in dummy, the defence could only make the ♡A.

Any list of all-time tops can only be a subjective opinion. I have told the truth, but have I told the whole truth? What about the failure to distinguish between Priday and Rodrigue? Even I must sometimes temper candour with diplomacy.

The fickle goddess

Whether you regard the Goddess of Chance with affection or distrust, luck indisputably plays an important part in match play as well as rubber bridge.

Some duplicate players fondly imagine that their game is a pure test of skill. How wrong they are. I have learned from bitter experience that you cannot win any pairs event, especially in a field of mixed quality, without your share of luck.

Multiple teams events afford a further refutation of the fallacy. It is only long head to head team matches which provide reliable evidence of the relative skill of the contestants. The evidence may be reliable, but as I shall demonstrate, it is far from conclusive.

This hand occurred in a vital European championship match between Britain and Italy some years ago.

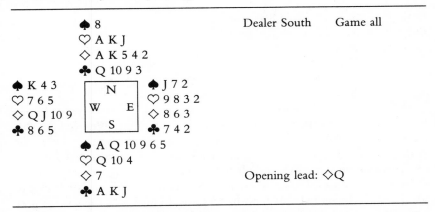

Both sides reached the ungainly contract of six no trumps. To be fair, the high point count, the two long suits and the duplication in hearts, combine to make it difficult to stay within one's depth. In both rooms, West led the ◇Q. It is obvious that declarer must play on spades hoping to establish the suit for only one loser. The Italian South played a spade to the ♠10. Bravo, Signor! The British declarer finessed the ♠Q. Bad luck!

On the surface, it appears a complete guess. Further consideration reveals that it is not. When the opposing spades are divided 3-3 it is indeed a complete toss up between the finesse of the ♠10 and ♠Q. But when the spades are divided 4-2 we see that one choice is distinctly superior. Suppose that West has a doubleton honour. If he has ♠Kx declarer is bound to lose two tricks whichever way he plays, but if West has ♠Jx, the play of the ♠Q restricts the loss in the suit to one trick. Today any experienced international player would know the percentage play. It was truly unlucky to lose a 26-point swing because of an opponent's ignorance.

The next hand decided a critical match in the Spingold trophy, one of America's two major knock-out events.

161

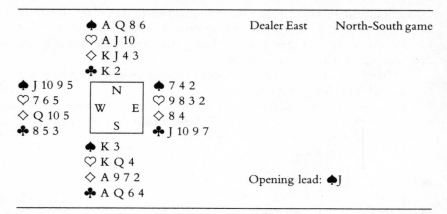

♠ A Q 8 6
♡ A J 10
◇ K J 4 3
♣ K 2

Dealer East   North–South game

♠ J 10 9 5
♡ 7 6 5
◇ Q 10 5
♣ 8 5 3

♠ 7 4 2
♡ 9 8 3 2
◇ 8 4
♣ J 10 9 7

♠ K 3
♡ K Q 4
◇ A 9 7 2
♣ A Q 6 4

Opening lead: ♠J

In the closed room the favourites bid to six no trumps. West led the ♠J. Declarer could count three tricks in spades, hearts and clubs, making nine in all. If he could make three diamond tricks the slam was assured. He won the first trick with the ♠K and played the ◇2 to the ◇K. He returned the ◇3 and when East followed with the ◇8 he contributed the ◇9, losing to West's ◇10. Provided that the suit was not divided 5–0, this line of play would guarantee three diamond tricks, regardless of the distribution.

In the open room the underdogs stumbled into the bad contract of seven diamonds. At IMP scoring, it is reasonable to bid a grand slam if the odds are 17–13 in your favour, as compared with the 2–1 on required to make the contract a sound proposition at rubber bridge. On this hand the grand slam is approximately 2–1 against. As you can see, with the diamonds lying favourably, there was no difficulty in making 13 tricks.

The losers took their defeat with good natured resignation. Only one thing rankled, which the declarer in the closed room explained: 'I don't mind the guy bidding and making a lucky grand slam, if only he had played it correctly, but he didn't. He just bashed out the ◇A and took the finesse.'

If you have to play that suit for no loser, you must start with a small diamond to dummy's ◇J, because of this possible distribution:

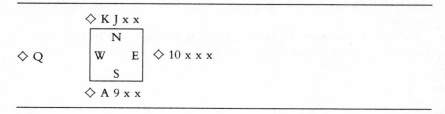

◇ K J x x

◇ Q

◇ 10 x x x

◇ A 9 x x

If your first move is to cash the $\diamond$A, you lose an unnecessary trick to East's $\diamond$10. If East has the singleton $\diamond$Q you cannot avoid losing a trick. I hope you will not find yourself in a grand slam with such a tenuous trump suit, but if you do, at least you will know how to play it.

My overdone Goulash

The Portland Club, responsible for drafting contract bridge rules, is also recognized as the ultimate court in any dispute that arises at rubber bridge, where it fulfils an equivalent function to the House of Lords sitting as a court of justice. The American Contract Bridge League accepts the Portland's authority, without attempting to conceal its feeling that the Portland's power stems from a particularly English anachronism.

The American objection can be partially explained by considering the special form of bridge played at the Portland. With the exception of an artificial two club opening, *no conventions are permitted.*

From time to time, I am lucky enough to be invited to one of the club's guest evenings. Over the champagne, my friends explain: 'You can't lose in this company.'

The subtle propaganda continues during the excellent dinner, invariably accompanied by distinguished wines. By now the expert guests are in the proper frame of mind.

Superficially, the opposition does not appear too formidable, but one deplorable result follows another. Your partner passes your forcing bid, and on the very next hand looks disappointed when you pass his sign-off. An opponent makes a stupendous underbid, the guile of which you appreciate only as his partner drops two tricks in the play.

Already demoralized, you pass your partner's opening no-trump bid. 'Goulie, Goulie,' your opponents cry, as if it were an Indian war chant. A moment's lapse of concentration has led you to forget this survival from the torture chamber of the Spanish inquisition.

For those who have never played Goulashes, I should explain that the cards, which are not shuffled, are dealt in two lots of five and one lot of three. There are those who like Goulashes because of the fiery distribution. There are those who, in Goulashes, show great cunning in the bidding and some admirable skill in the play. As is well known at the Portland, I belong to neither group.

	♠ 4			Goulash	Rubber bridge
♠ Void	♡ J 10 9 8 7 6 4 3		♠ K Q J 10 9 8 6 5	Game all	
♡ A Q	◇ Void		♡ K 5 2	Dealer North	
◇ Q 6 5 2	♣ A K 10 2		◇ 4		
♣ Q J 9 8 6 4 3			♣ 7		

```
            ♠ 4
            ♡ J 10 9 8 7 6 4 3
            ◇ Void
            ♣ A K 10 2
♠ Void      ┌─────────┐   ♠ K Q J 10 9 8 6 5
♡ A Q       │    N    │   ♡ K 5 2
◇ Q 6 5 2   │ W     E │   ◇ 4
♣ Q J 9 8 6 4 3 │  S  │   ♣ 7
            └─────────┘
            ♠ A 7 3 2
            ♡ Void
            ◇ A K J 10 9 8 7 3
            ♣ 5
```

West	**North**	**East**	**South**
R. Mc-	Jim	K.	The
Alpine	Slater	Wagg	Mug
—	3♡	4♠	5◇
Dble	NB	NB	NB

Opening lead: ♣Q

The method of dealing, coupled with the absence of a shuffle, increases the probability of wild distributions. Although some Goulash experts (possibly looking to the future?) say my call of five diamonds was defensible, I think it was typically imprudent. After all, how did I hope to dispose of my three small spades?

McAlpine had no doubts. He doubled, and led the ♣Q as Slater put down his dummy with polite resignation. It was easy to see my bidding was wrong, for my heart void coupled with partner's ♣A would surely be sufficient to defeat four spades.

I won with dummy's ♣A, ruffed a heart with the ◇7, and then cashed the ◇K. When I played the ◇J, McAlpine won with the ◇Q, and seeing that dummy was devoid of entries, got off play with the ♡A, which I ruffed with the ◇8. I cashed the ◇A and put McAlpine on play by exiting with the ◇3 to his ◇6.

'A hundred honours, partner', I said apologetically, as McAlpine blamed himself for not retaining the precious ◇2.

There is a considerable case for excluding conventions from rubber bridge. It makes an exciting game, and sets a premium on good judgement. I remain less convinced that it is right to bar calls such as cue bids which, although not natural, rely for their interpretation on common sense rather than convention.

To complete the record, there is, as I discovered to my cost, one other permitted convention. Normally, you are expected to lead the K from the AK. In a Goulash, you should lead the Ace. Ignorantly, I failed to do so.

'Surely you knew that', said Jim Slater.

'Is that the convention?' I asked.

'It is not a convention', he replied, 'it is . . . er . . . a well established custom'.

Finding the ideal partner

Wanted. Partner capable of learning and remembering complicated system. Must be a good defender.

Available now. Expert dummy player, sparkling defender, aggressive bidder. Former partner gone abroad (I hope).

These are imaginary samples of my Bridge Computer Dating Service. I must admit that for the present there is a snag. Whereas a balding man with a paunch could scarcely describe himself as 'young and athletic', the bridge looking glass is well known for its flattery.

The importance of partnership understanding in both tournament and rubber bridge can hardly be exaggerated. If you study the famous partnerships, you will often find that the most successful have worked on a 'pitcher catcher' basis. The combination of two brilliant 'pitchers' may produce some sparkling coups but will suffer too many expensive losses. When two 'catchers' play together, their inherent caution leads to underbidding. Their losses may be few and far between but so will be their gains.

In the late 1950s, Reese and Schapiro were regarded as one of the most dangerous pairs in the world. Schapiro supplied the thrust, Reese the inpenetrable straight bat. The picture was the same with the Italians. Forquet was an immaculate foil for Garozzo's virtuosity, and Avarelli's dogged accuracy was a safety net for Belladonna's fearless acrobatics.

This hand, at World Championship level, shows how damaging partnership misunderstandings can be. The match was France v USA, in the round robin of the World Championships in Taiwan, 1971.

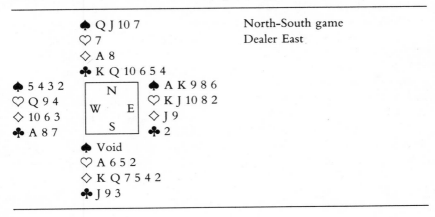

```
                  ♠ Q J 10 7              North-South game
                  ♡ 7                     Dealer East
                  ◇ A 8
                  ♣ K Q 10 6 5 4
   ♠ 5 4 3 2    ┌─────────┐    ♠ A K 9 8 6
   ♡ Q 9 4      │    N    │    ♡ K J 10 8 2
   ◇ 10 6 3     │ W     E │    ◇ J 9
   ♣ A 8 7      │    S    │    ♣ 2
                └─────────┘
                  ♠ Void
                  ♡ A 6 5 2
                  ◇ K Q 7 5 4 2
                  ♣ J 9 3
```

In the open room, the Americans had been doubled in five clubs, which they had made with an overtrick. French supporters were not totally despondent, because if their North-South pair could bid the slam, France would still gain on the board.

This was the bidding in the closed room, with France North-South.

West	North	East	South
—	—	1 ♠	2 ◇
2 ♠	Dble	NB	2 NT
NB	3 NT	NB	NB
NB	—	—	—

This ungainly contract went three down, so France lost a total of 1,250 points, equivalent to 15 IMPs. South's bid of 2NT was intended to convey that he had four hearts. He argued that it could not be a natural bid, for with such a hand he would either pass the double or bid 3NT. The loss did not prevent France from qualifying for the final, but the French captain did not allow the pair who had made this unhappy muddle to play for the first 80 boards of the final. At the time it was suggested that France lost the Championship because of fatigue, so it is imposible to calculate the real cost of this misunderstanding.

S.J. Simon gave the best recipe for success at rubber bridge. In his classic, '*Why you lose at Bridge*,' he wrote: 'Try for the best result possible. Not the best possible result.' In other words, be satisfied with half a loaf.

There are many opportunities for skilled and delicate bidding, but the good psychologist will be careful not to stray outside his partner's bidding vocabulary. On this deal, which is a distant echo of my first hand, East was an expert playing with a partner who was normally reliable.

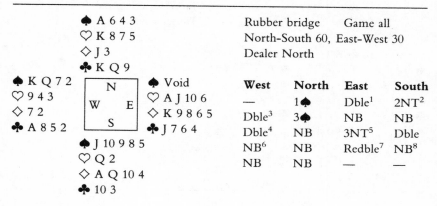

```
              ♠ A 6 4 3
              ♡ K 8 7 5
              ◇ J 3
              ♣ K Q 9
♠ K Q 7 2    ┌─────────┐    ♠ Void
♡ 9 4 3      │    N    │    ♡ A J 10 6
◇ 7 2        │ W     E │    ◇ K 9 8 6 5
♣ A 8 5 2    │    S    │    ♣ J 7 6 4
              └─────────┘
              ♠ J 10 9 8 5
              ♡ Q 2
              ◇ A Q 10 4
              ♣ 10 3
```

Rubber bridge   Game all
North-South 60, East-West 30
Dealer North

West	North	East	South
—	1 ♠	Dble[1]	2NT[2]
Dble[3]	3 ♠	NB	NB
Dble[4]	NB	3NT[5]	Dble
NB[6]	NB	Redble[7]	NB[8]
NB	NB	—	—

166

1 Obviously speculative, but justifiable at the score.

2 Describing a hand with the values for a genuine raise to 3♠ as opposed to a barrage raise.

3 A legitimate move to show some strength.

4 This is a mistake. When all the players are bidding it is evident that East's double must be based almost entirely on shape. K Q 7 2 is an inadequate trump holding to make a unilateral decision.

5 Preparing the parachute.

6 West should bid 4♣. When South doubles 3NT, there cannot be sufficient high cards in the pack for East's 3NT to be a natural bid.

7 West's pass of 3NT doubled should have been a warning.

8 Roman candle.

I dislike violence and the sight of blood, so I will not describe the play. It cost 2,800.

Cheating by degrees

Cheating at cards has carried its own special stigma since the Tranby Croft scandal. At bridge, the spectrum of 'cheating' extends from the veniality of a parking offence to the felony of conspiracy.

There are three distinct degrees of unacceptable behaviour. First, the telltale mannerisms or hesitations and the marked changes in the emphasis or tempo with which a player makes a bid.

'Everyone knows that when John moves his chair back, he always has a good hand.'

'Harry leaves you in no doubt when *his* doubles are for penalties.'

'Tom has developed his two and three-quarter spade raise to a fine art.'

If you told the culprits they were cheating, they would be horrified. For the most part, they are totally unconscious of their habits. Certainly they lack dishonest intent. In my experience, few amateurs can intone their bids in the unaltering pitch of a chorister's plainsong.

The second, more serious form of abuse is restricted to multiple duplicate events, where the same hands are played at a number of tables. Undeniably a few unprincipled players seek to obtain illicit knowledge of the hands they have yet to play. In an effort to combat these malpractices, the American Contract Bridge League has introduced closed circuit television at some tournaments. This has proved to be a controversial move, its opponents arguing that any benefits are outweighed by the sinister Big Brother atmosphere. Regrettably, I feel that multiple events will always be bedevilled by the occasional villain whom no amount of security can forestall.

The last and most pernicious form of cheating is the deliberate collusion between two players to exchange signals by a pre-arranged code. Luckily there have been few such cases over the years, and only one which I can remember being conclusively proved.

There are, I believe, some good reasons for the rarity. Perhaps I am naive, but I believe that, for most people, to win by fraud would be to rob the game of its essential satisfaction, the demonstration of their superior intellectual skill. For the few who would be sufficiently amoral, there are some practical deterrents. An 18-handicap golfer cannot become scratch overnight. At bridge, if a pair were to improve too dramatically it would obviously invite close scrutiny. Again, if an indifferent dummy player shows an uncanny instinct in both bidding and defence, he must expect the occasional suspicious glance.

The final stumbling block is called 'the area of tolerance'. Suppose two good players have devised a code which escapes visual detection, they cannot use it all the time. There must be a logical explanation for their 'flair'. Bridge already makes considerable demands on a player's concentration. If, in addition to covertly emitting and receiving the illicit signals, the cheat has to reflect whether he has a legitimate excuse to take advantage of them, he will hardly retain sufficient concentration to follow suit.

The American player Peter Winkler raises a provocative point in an article in *Bridge Magazine*. This hand will introduce the theme.

```
                ♠ A 8
                ♡ K 8 7 6 5
                ♢ Q 10 9 8 7
                ♣ A
♠ K Q J 10 3   ┌───────┐   ♠ 9 7 6 5 2
♡ 2            │   N   │   ♡ 4 3
♢ 2            │ W   E │   ♢ A 6 5 4
♣ 10 9 8 7 6 2 │   S   │   ♣ J 3
               └───────┘
                ♠ 4
                ♡ A Q J 10 9
                ♢ K J 3
                ♣ K Q 5 4
```

| | Teams | Game all | |
| | Dealer South | | |

West	North	East	South
—	—	—	1♡
NB	2♢	NB	3♣
NB	4♡	NB	4NT[1]
NB	5♡[2]	NB	6♡
NB	NB	NB	—

1 Roman Blackwood.
2 Two aces of the same colour.

Before he leads, West asks, as he is entitled to do, the meaning of North's five hearts. South quite properly explains that it shows two aces of the same colour. South knows that on this hand his partner has the ♣A and ♠A. The luckless West has to find a lead. Who can blame him for surmising that the bidding suggests that North has the two red aces, in which case to lead a singleton would be futile. No one has implied that the extra knowledge that South possesses is improper, or that he is under any obligation to disclose the identity of North's aces to West.

But Winkler's article suggests that there are many opportunities, both in the bidding and in the play, where a partnership can have a *legitimate* understanding of which they alone have the code. This hand illustrates one such area.

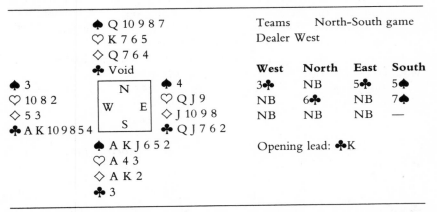

	♠ Q 10 9 8 7		
	♡ K 7 6 5		
	◇ Q 7 6 4		
	♣ Void		

Teams   North-South game
Dealer West

West	North	East	South
3♣	NB	5♣	5♠
NB	6♣	NB	7♠
NB	NB	NB	—

Opening lead: ♣K

West leads the ♣K on which East plays the ♣Q, and South ruffs in dummy. We see that there are only 12 tricks, because the diamonds do not break, and there is no squeeze. In practice, East will have to find some awkward discards. But suppose West could signal his distribution in the red suits? Yes, that would be fine on this hand, but could be fatal if the information allowed declarer to play double dummy.

This is Winkler's suggestion. When the opening lead is ruffed, signals are determined by which defender possesses the lowest card in the suit — here the ♣2. If it is West, then the signals will be normal. If it is East they will be reversed, i.e. 'untrue'. The defenders alone have the key to the code.

As I write, it is uncertain whether the World Bridge Laws Commission will permit these signals to be used★. Perhaps they should seek the advice of the Inland Revenue, which is used to making the fine distinction between the commendable art of tax avoidance and the horrors of tax evasion.

★ These signals are not permitted in the United Kingdom.

Commons forced to bow to the Lords

The annual bridge match between the Lords and the Commons was held at the Inn on the Park, London W1. The Commons, possibly smarting from a succession of defeats, introduced some heavy parliamentary guns, notably Mr John Silkin. Understandably, the Duke of Atholl was content to rely on a team of trusted and proved lieutenants.

It was difficult not to feel sorry for the Commons. They reminded me of a fragile English batting side exposed to a hostile Australian attack on a wicket which still retained its early moisture. They lost the first rubber by 3,790–380, and the second by 1,490–250. After only two rubbers their 'innings' was already in tatters, with the score standing at the Lords 5,280, the Commons 630 (the equivalent of 72 for 8 at cricket).

This was an early Commons 'dismissal', which no doubt Richie Benaud would have described with lip-smacking sympathy.

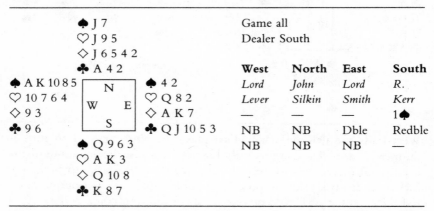

	♠ J 7	
	♡ J 9 5	
	◇ J 6 5 4 2	
	♣ A 4 2	

Game all
Dealer South

West	North	East	South
Lord	*John*	*Lord*	*R.*
Lever	*Silkin*	*Smith*	*Kerr*
—	—	—	1♠
NB	NB	Dble	Redble
NB	NB	NB	—

♠ A K 10 8 5
♡ 10 7 6 4
◇ 9 3
♣ 9 6

♠ 4 2
♡ Q 8 2
◇ A K 7
♣ Q J 10 5 3

♠ Q 9 6 3
♡ A K 3
◇ Q 10 8
♣ K 8 7

A most satisfactory auction for Lord Lever, who has earned his sobriquet, 'The Hammer of the Commons'. It is not clear whether Mr Kerr's redouble was a cry for help. If it was, it fell on deaf ears.

Declarer did not make quite the best of this unappetizing contract, with the result that the Lords inflicted a penalty of 1,600.

Possibly Mr Kerr and Mr Silkin had been unnerved by the menacing accuracy of the Lords' attack on the previous hand.

```
                ♠ J 10 5 2              North–South game
                ♡ 10 7                  Dealer East
                ◇ 7 5 3 2
                ♣ Q 5 4
```

				West	North	East	South
♠ A K Q 3		N	♠ 8	*Lord*	*John*	*Lord*	*R.*
♡ A Q J 6 5	W		E	*Lever*	*Silkin*	*Smith*	*Kerr*
◇ 4		S	♡ K 9 8 3 2	—	—	NB	1◇
♣ A 7 2			◇ 10 8 6	2◇	NB	2♡	NB
			♣ K J 10 6	4♡	NB	5♣[1]	NB
	♠ 9 7 6 4			6♡	NB	NB	NB
	♡ 4						
	◇ A K Q J 9						
	♣ 9 8 3						

1 An excellent bid by the former president of the Royal College of Surgeons, demonstrating that his diagnosis at the bridge table is as accurate as it is in the operating theatre.

To prove that robes of ermine cloak men of flesh and blood, the Earl of Birkenhead and Lord Smith gave us this spectacular misunderstanding.

```
                ♠ Q 9 8                 Love all
                ♡ J 4                   Dealer West
                ◇ 8 6
                ♣ J 9 6 5 4 3
```

				West	North	East	South
♠ A K J 4 3		N	♠ 10 7 6 5	*Lord*			*Lord*
♡ 10 7 6	W		E		*Birkenhead*		*Smith*
◇ 4 3		S	♡ K 9 8	1♠	NB	NB	2♠
♣ K 10 8			◇ 10 9 7	NB	3♣	NB	3♠
	♠ 2		♣ Q 7 2	Dble	NB	NB	Redble
	♡ A Q 5 3 2			NB	NB	NB	—
	◇ A K Q J 5 2						
	♣ A						

Strange to relate, if declarer times the play to perfection he can make eight tricks in this weird contract. As it was, he conceded a penalty of 600.

The Commons fought bravely to the end, but they could not overcome the enormous early deficit. The final margin was 11,490–5,760.

Perhaps the next Parliament, irrespective of its political complexion, will provide the Commons with some new bridge faces to disturb the Lords' apparent invincibility.

Did you desert JR?

The BBC's first televised bridge match ended with Great Britain withstanding a sustained American counter-attack to win by the narrow margin of 7 IMPs. More important than the result was the reaction of players throughout the country to bridge on television. The bare statistics reveal that the average audience was one and a quarter million. As this was achieved in competition with rival attractions such as *Dallas*, it must be considered a gratifying response.

I am grateful to those readers who wrote to me or the BBC offering constructive criticism. Obviously this first series had its imperfections.

The most frequent complaint was that the cards were difficult to see, especially in the diagrams illustrating the play. Apparently red presents particular problems on television, as the colour tends to 'run'. The obvious answer of enlarging the cards is impractical because the effect would be to make the screen appear cluttered.

Many viewers thought the play went too fast, making it hard to follow. Some said it was unnatural for the players to smile or alter their facial expression. But if one accepts the soliloquies it would surely be flat and unnatural for the players to intone their lines with a deadpan face. Others thought that by including some very elementary comments, the programme would irritate part of its committed audience of good bridge players.

Finally, there was the journalist who could see no merit in the series at all. I could not help thinking that it was lucky Marconi did not have to present his invention to such a critic, for it would surely have been dismissed in a sentence: 'Quite useless, it crackles'.

I make no apology for resurrecting the dramatic hand which finally decided the match because there were a number of interesting points that the commentator did not have time to mention.

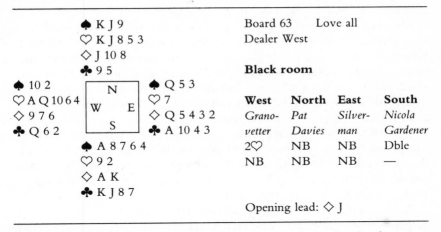

♠ K J 9
♡ K J 8 5 3
◇ J 10 8
♣ 9 5

♠ 10 2
♡ A Q 10 6 4
◇ 9 7 6
♣ Q 6 2

N
W E
S

♠ Q 5 3
♡ 7
◇ Q 5 4 3 2
♣ A 10 4 3

♠ A 8 7 6 4
♡ 9 2
◇ A K
♣ K J 8 7

Board 63   Love all
Dealer West

Black room

West	North	East	South
Grano-	Pat	Silver-	Nicola
vetter	Davies	man	Gardener
2♡	NB	NB	Dble
NB	NB	NB	—

Opening lead: ◇ J

Two boards earlier the Americans had taken the lead for the first time when Silverman had made his contract of three clubs doubled, to earn a substantial swing. For that reason Granovetter was possibly imprudent to introduce a weak two bid on a five-card suit. South won the opening lead with the ◇K and cashed the ◇A, on which North contributed the ◇10, in an attempt to attract a spade switch.

South preferred the safe continuation of the ♡9. West took the ♡A and continued with the ♡10. When North won with the ♡J it was her turn to find the spade switch. Possibly reflecting that South might have taken the first trick with the ◇A followed by the ◇K instead of the other way round, she switched to a club, enabling Granovetter to save what could have been a crucial trick. 500 to Great Britain.

White room

West	North	East	South
Rodrigue	Jacqui Mitchell	Flint	Gail Moss
NB	NB	NB	1 ♠
NB	2 ♠	NB	3 ♣
NB	4 ♠	NB	NB
NB	—	—	—

Opening lead: ◇ 7

The opening lead was consistent with our style of leading the middle of three small cards. Sometimes, as here, a player will be unsure of his partner's holding in the suit. It was perfectly possible that West had ♢K97, in which case the failure to play the ♢Q could cost the defence its diamond trick. Luckily I guessed correctly when I played the ♢2. Declarer won the trick and reasonably played a heart, but unwisely selected the ♡2. When Rodrigue won with the ♡A he *knew* that my ♡7 must be a singleton, for in this setting it is mandatory to echo with a doubleton. If declarer had played the ♡9, concealing the ♡2, Rodrigue would have been forced to guess the distribution.

When Rodrigue continued with a second heart, declarer played the ♡K, a doubtful decision because good players usually duck when they hold the Ace unless they hold the Queen as well. Notice that if declarer had played the ♡J and subsequently guessed the position of the ♣A, she could have made ten tricks and won the match!

When I ruffed the ♡K, some players would have been rattled by the calamitous turn of events. Not Gail Moss. She won my diamond return and made a very fine if unsuccessful, attempt to recover. *She finessed the* ♣J. Why? The best hope was to find me with ♣AQ10x and originally three trumps. To take advantage of that distribution she needed two entries to dummy. That apparently purposeless finesse was a far-sighted play aimed at creating a vital extra entry.

To summarise my final thoughts on the BBC's brave experiment, I cannot improve on the brevity of racing jargon.

'Well made. Scope. Slowly into stride. Ran on well. Sure to improve'.

Gaps to fill between the acts

Painswick is a charming village set in the undulating Cotswolds, near Stroud. For those who believe that the English breakfast, personal service, and food and wine served with care and pride are all things of the past, the Painswick Hotel represents a delightful contradiction.

During the last week in August, the hotel became the headquarters of the film unit who were shooting the bridge programme *Grand Slam* at Painswick House nearby. The after-dinner entertainment consisted of croquet on the floodlit lawn and bridge. The croquet would have been unrecognizable to those accustomed to the decorum of Hurlingham, the American girls insisting that it is legal to place a foot on one ball and that there was no penalty for going off the lawn. Worse still, Jeremy James, the presenter, felt impelled to act as a moving handicap by using his shadow to distract the favourites.

The bridge was played in a similarly light-hearted vein. On the hand I shall describe, West was Mark Patterson the executive producer, playing with Neil Silverman, the American expert. Silverman played under the handicap that he was not allowed to look at his cards until the bidding was completed. Patterson, if unlikely to represent Great Britain, played with great cunning under exisiting conditions, making jump overcalls on short suits on the reasonable premise that his partner Silverman would be less deceived than the opposition. North was Joyce Silverman and South was Peter Bazalgette, the producer. The last rubber had as usual dragged on for some time.

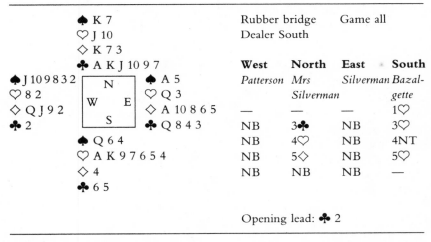

	♠ K 7		Rubber bridge	Game all		
	♡ J 10		Dealer South			
	◇ K 7 3					
	♣ A K J 10 9 7		**West**	**North**	**East**	**South**
♠ J 10 9 8 3 2		♠ A 5	*Patterson*	*Mrs*	*Silverman*	*Bazal-*
♡ 8 2		♡ Q 3		*Silverman*		*gette*
◇ Q J 9 2		◇ A 10 8 6 5	—	—	—	1♡
♣ 2		♣ Q 8 4 3	NB	3♣	NB	3♡
	♠ Q 6 4		NB	4♡	NB	4NT
	♡ A K 9 7 6 5 4		NB	5◇	NB	5♡
	◇ 4		NB	NB	NB	—
	♣ 6 5					

Opening lead: ♣ 2

Bazalgette immediately regretted his enterprise, but the thought of an early start the next day made him even more determined to make the game. Silverman felt confident of defeating the contract when he found his hand contained such an unexpected wealth of high cards.

A natural line would be to draw trumps, establish the clubs and rely on the ♠K to provide an entry. Bazalgette found a slight improvement. After drawing trumps and establishing the clubs, he played the ♠Q, which was ducked all round! When Bazalgette continued with a second spade, Silverman was end-played. He could not avoid conceding the lead to dummy, enabling declarer to dispose of his spade.

When I asked Bazalgette whether he had thought of overtaking his ♠Q with dummy's ♠K, he replied: 'Of course not — Mark very rarely ducks after 1.30 am, and if he does, he doesn't do it "furtively", if you know what I mean.'

175